Help Yourself

John M. Lembo, Ed.D.

Argus Communications
1974
Niles, Illinois

Library of Congress Catalog
Card Number: 73-94484

International Standard Book
Number: 0-913592-27-7

Contents

To the reader

The aphorisms illustrated in this book
have been selected by the publisher.
Many of them are consistent with the
author's philosophy, some are not.
They are to be read with a searching
mind. Their purpose is to help the
reader discover his or her own beliefs,
evaluate them by reflecting carefully
on the author's ideas, and move toward
developing a more realistic philosophy
of life.

J.M.L.

Foreword

I am delighted to introduce John M. Lembo's *Help Yourself* to the reading public—mainly because I think that it is a valuable addition to the psychological literature and that it will prove helpful to almost everyone who carefully reads and thinks about its contents. Professor Lembo has written a remarkably lucid and understandable book on rational self-counseling and has included practical details that are sadly missing from most other similarly oriented works in this area.

Help Yourself beautifully exemplifies the new trend that has taken place in the handling of emotional problems, a trend that is causing something of a revolution in the field of psychology. Let me briefly mention some of the main aspects of this revolutionary approach.

First of all, after being foolishly divorced from philosophy for almost a century, psychotherapy is now re-aligning itself within a philosophic fold. Peter A. Bertocci, in reviewing the work of Isidor Chein and Gordon Allport, incisively points out that they, following the spirit of William James, realize "that a psychology of personality is at the same time a philosophy of personality." Mildred Newman and Bernard Berkowitz, in their best-selling book, *How To Be Your Own Best Friend,* presumably write as practicing psychoanalysts but actually eschew almost entirely the psycho-analytic or psychodynamic position and promul-gate a distinctly philosophic approach to solving emotional problems. Outstanding contemporary psychologists, such as Viktor Frankl and Rollo May, are largely philosophically oriented; and my own writings, for the last two decades, have upheld the position that human beliefs, values, and philosophies (rather than only their early experiences) importantly determine how they emote and act.

Secondly, *Help Yourself* re-promulgates the idea that psychological help can largely consist of *self*-help. My colleagues and I, at the Institute for Advanced Study in Rational Psychotherapy in New York City, have used this principle to good advantage in our work with individual and group therapy clients, as well as with students and participants in our regular public talks, courses, seminars and workshops. Almost everyone who comes to the Institute is encouraged to read various self-management pamphlets and books or to listen to self-help recordings. We have consistently found that this kind of *bibliotherapy* is exceptionally beneficial, and both speeds up and enhances the therapeutic process. We also have literally hundreds of unsolicited communications from people all over the world who have read and listened to the material we distribute and who insist that, without any contact with a professional therapist, they have considerably changed undesirable personality characteristics by this form of bibliotherapy. Professor Lembo obviously believes that books like his can be valuable for people in psychotherapy as well as for those who are trying to solve some of their problems on their own. Our experience indicates that he is almost certainly right.

Thirdly, *Help Yourself* emphasizes the importance of homework assignments in dealing with emotional problems. I think I got the idea for such assignments from several previous writers in the fields of human happiness and mental health, including Bertrand Russell, Alexander

We become
persons
only by making
personal
decisions.

Herzberg, and Andrew Salter. Also, when I was in my late teens and early twenties, I systematically carried out some thought-changing and self-disciplining homework assignments on myself, and thereby became quite convinced of their efficacy. More recently, a whole host of cognitive-behavior therapists, including Albert Bandura, Frederick H. Kanfer, Thomas J. D'Zurilla, Donald H. Meichenbaum, Marvin R. Goldfried, and Michael Merbaum, have emphasized the importance and effectiveness of self-management procedures. Professor Lembo logically follows this tradition and creatively adds to it.

For these and other reasons, *Help Yourself* is truly a revolutionary book. It endorses and extends the new emphasis on active-directive, cognitive-behavior, philosophic psychotherapy. Not that it presents any panaceas. As I have pointed out in *Humanistic Psychotherapy: The Rational-Emotive Approach,* all therapies and self-help procedures have their definite limitations. "Human beings are practically never completely uncondemning and tolerant. Even when they are helped significantly by a psychotherapeutic process, they tend to slip back to some degree into their old patterns of undisciplined and overemotional behavior. To remain even reasonably rational and not self-defeating, they have to work hard and long, and they frequently fail to do this." Professor Lembo's book of course does not assure that its readers will work hard and long to help themselves surmount some of their main emotional hangups. But it certainly shows them how to work, if they really want to do this!

Albert Ellis, Ph.D.

Preface

The greatest tragedy of twentieth century America is not the great wars or earthquakes or floods but the failure of people to manage their personal lives in productive and meaningful ways. This greatest of tragedies is revealed in the alarming rate of suicide among today's young people. It is revealed in the tons of tranquilizers and the millions of gallons of alcohol that are consumed each year. It is revealed in the widespread use of marijuana and other mind-expanding drugs. It is revealed in the loss of meaning that men and women experience in their work, their relationships and their leisure time. Clearly, millions of people are anxious, confused and unable to direct their lives in constructive and personally satisfying ways.

Wanting to experience a more meaningful and satisfying life, many people are turning to formal psychotherapy. However, available evidence suggests that they have no assurance that they will learn to direct their lives in more constructive ways by seeing a psychotherapist. While some who undergo psychotherapy report significant improvement, many report no improvement at

To **L**ive
is
the rarest thing
in the world.

Most people exist,
that is all.

all, and still others report an actual increase in the number or intensity of disabling symptoms. In view of the fact that time spent in psychotherapy is often long, that costs are usually high and that results are almost always unpredictable, unhappy people want realistic alternatives to psychotherapy.

Help Yourself is one such alternative. This aid to self-management maintains that people direct their lives by the way they think and talk to themselves and that they can lead reasonably happy lives by using rational self-help techniques with regularity. It is important to understand, however, that people will not learn to direct their lives more effectively simply by *reading* about self-management theories and strategies. No written guide, or person, can, for all the money in the world, *give* people the skills to live more productively. They will learn to lead more meaningful and satisfying lives only by systematically *implementing* self-help techniques each day.

ACKNOWLEDGMENTS

I am indebted to many people for the ideas that make up this book. While *Help Yourself* developed through my own experience, many outstanding past and present philosophers, psychotherapists and social thinkers have been my teachers. I want especially to credit the writings of Albert Ellis and Viktor Frankl for much of the philosophical framework of this book.

I am grateful to Cande O'Donnell, John O'Donnell and Richard Olds who carefully read the manuscript and offered many helpful suggestions. I give special thanks to my wife, Judy, who often postponed the pursuit of her own interests to type several drafts of the manuscript.

Help
Yourself

one

Talking
to ourselves

one

Every waking moment we talk to ourselves about the things we experience. Our self-talk, *the thoughts that we communicate to ourselves,* in turn control the way we feel and act. For example, if a young woman sees someone point a gun at her and she thinks and tells herself that her life is in danger, she most likely will become very frightened and probably try to flee. This example of experiencing, talking to oneself, feeling and acting may be diagrammed in the following way.

Experience   See a gun pointed at oneself

Self-talk   "It's a real gun. He is going to kill me."

Feeling   Fear

Action   Try to escape.

The most important point about this example is that the woman's self-talk controlled her feelings and actions. If upon seeing a gun pointed at her, the woman had told herself different thoughts, she would have felt and acted differently. If she had told herself that the gun was made of milk chocolate and that her life was not in any danger, she would not have become frightened and she would not have tried to escape.

These observations suggest the first important insight for helping ourselves:

> It is not the events
> that we encounter
> but the thoughts we tell ourselves
> that determine
> how we feel and act.

We can find evidence to support this insight by observing the behavior of another. A man who tells himself and others that women are sex objects tends to treat women accordingly. A woman who believes that men control everything will usually blame men for her problems and unhappiness. A white person who thinks that "niggers" are a serious threat to his economic survival often treats black people as enemies. And a black person who believes that "whitey" must pay for all the discrimination against black people is likely to be hostile and sometimes violent toward white people.

The entire history of humankind is testimony that the thoughts people tell themselves determine the way they behave. The doctor of the past who believed that bloodletting would provide the cure persisted in this practice despite the fact that patients died before his very eyes. The clergyman who was convinced that bizarre behavior was the result of being possessed by the devil devised the cruelest methods to drive the devil out. The patriot who told himself that he was a member of the master race enslaved others and treated them as less than human.

3

Regardless of the kind of personal or interpersonal behavior that is studied, there is evidence that the thoughts people tell themselves determine the way they feel and act.

This principle in turn suggests a second important insight for helping ourselves:

It is not our experiences
but our self-talk
that determines
the meaning of our lives.

Meaning does not reside in events or situations. Nor can it be *found*. *Meaning is created* by what we tell ourselves about our experiences. Whether people live in different parts of the world or in the same neighborhood, they often have similar experiences regarding work, marriage, children and other aspects of life. But because each person communicates different thoughts to himself or herself about a given experience, each person gives a different meaning to an experience that is common to many people. If a child darts into the street and is struck and killed by a car, each observer gives a different meaning to the incident. One person tells herself, "The car is the most monstrous thing invented by man." Another insists, "It was the child's fault." A third asks, "What kind of God would let an innocent child be killed like that?" And a fourth may say, "That girl won't have to put up with her drunken father anymore." Thus, experiences do not *hold* meaning. Meaning is *given* to them, and the kind of meaning given is determined by what we tell ourselves.

The **M**eaning
of life
is out there somewhere,

and it is up to each
to find it
for **H**imself.

Self-talk may be either rational (true *and* logical) or irrational (false *or* illogical). When a student fails a test, she may tell herself either, "I'm a fallible human being"; or, "I am a failure and no good." When a secretary is lied to by *one* of the many people she encounters during her working day, she may say either, "Occasionally a person will lie"; or, "People are deceptive and manipulative." A businessman who experiences a great disappointment in his ventures may tell himself either, "Things are not always the way I would like them to be"; or, "This is a cruel and horrible world."

Rational and irrational self-talk produces different consequences which can be observed. A mother who believes that her son is an imperfect person just like herself, that he is prone to behaving in illogical and inefficient ways at times, and that his faulty thinking and self-talk explain why he often does foolish things, will be able to understand her son's behavior and respond to it without making herself angry. On the other hand, if she tells herself that her son is a rotten brat who is ruining her life, she will not only fail to understand her son's behavior, but she will be setting herself up for open warfare.

Similarly, a policeman who believes that, just like himself, a long-haired protestor is a fallible human being who has some true and false ideas about himself and the world and whose self-talk explains why he is protesting, will be able to understand the protestor's behavior and respond to it without making himself upset. On the other hand, a policeman who tells himself that the long-haired protestor is a drug-crazed, irresponsible piece of garbage and a threat to society, will fail to understand the protestor's behavior and will be setting himself up for an emotional upset and perhaps a dangerous conflict. These observations suggest a third important insight for helping ourselves:

> **Rational self-talk**
> **creates understanding**
> **and prevents emotional upsets**
> **and interpersonal conflicts**
> **while**
> **irrational self-talk**
> **prevents understanding**
> **and creates emotional upsets**
> **and interpersonal conflicts.**

The thoughts that we tell ourselves are not genetically determined. As Albert Ellis points out in *A Guide to Rational Living,* our self-talk is *learned* from parents, teachers, church officials and others in our culture. Because it is learned, *we can tell ourselves either rational or irrational thoughts.* Consider the following:

We can tell ourselves rational or irrational thoughts about *the way things are.* We can believe that we are competent but fallible or incompetent and worthless; that most people are basically responsible and constructive or irresponsible and destructive; that life is a series of opportunities for self-fulfillment or a series of mazes with dead ends.

Our thoughts about *the way things can be* can also be rational or irrational. We can be convinced that a modest degree of success can be achieved in our work or that it cannot; that realistic solutions can be found to our financial problems or that they cannot; that a reasonable degree of happiness can be experienced in our marriage or that it cannot.

In like manner, we can judge *the things that are of value* rationally or irrationally. We can tell ourselves that our friendships are more important than material success or that wealth and status are the more important things in life; that self-honesty is more desirable than social approval or that social approval is to be gained at all costs. And we can be rational or irrational in our convictions about *the way things need to be,* telling ourselves that we do not need to achieve perfection or that we must perform flawlessly in everything; that we do not always need to be pleased by our spouse or that our spouse must always satisfy our wants.

In addition, we can think rationally or irrationally about *the things that will happen to us* and insist that we will not be a failure if our boss fires us or that we will be a worthless no-account if we are dismissed from our job; that nothing catastrophic will happen if our parents die or that it will be horrible and unbearable if they do die. These observations suggest a fourth important insight for helping ourselves:

> **We may not have the power**
> **to control the events**
> **we encounter,**
> **but**
> **we can almost always**
> **tell ourselves rational thoughts**
> **about each of our experiences.**

9

This fourth insight leads to the basic thesis of this book:

> We have the ability
> to create a satisfying life
> for ourselves,
> and we will succeed in doing so
> if we rationally manage
> the thoughts we tell ourselves.

A self-fulfilling life may seem an impossibility when we consider all the irrationality in the world. Each day we observe widespread bigotry, inefficiency, violence and injustice, and we work and perhaps live with people who are thought-less, frustrating, malicious or disturbed. However, as Albert Ellis points out, "A human being in today's world does not *have* to be unhappy." If we intelligently discipline the way we think and talk to ourselves, we can live "a decidedly self-fulfilling, creative and emotionally satisfying life *even* in the highly unsatisfactory world of today."

The remainder of this book is about strategies for rationally managing the way we talk to ourselves about our lives. Specifically, rational techniques are described for pursuing goals, conducting relationships and dealing with unpleasant experiences. If we implement these rational techniques each day, we can gradually create more satisfying and conflict-free lives for ourselves.

two

Establishing and pursuing personal goals

two

As children, most of us were told by parents, church officials, teachers and others that we could give meaning to our lives by pursuing the things that *they* valued. Many of us may have interpreted the question, "How can I have a satisfying life?" to mean, "How do I achieve the things that other people believe are satisfying?" As a consequence, we may have spent most of our lives pursuing the things that are satisfying to other people but not to ourselves.

Today, many people in positions of authority—whether they be parents, teachers, politicians or businessmen—still try to convince us that their values are the ones to be pursued, that their beliefs about money, status, marriage, sex, religion and other things will give our life meaning. However, we are not hopelessly doomed to childhood dependency. We can talk rationally to ourselves about the goals that are in our best interest, and we can make realistic choices. The following questions may be helpful in establishing and pursuing personal goals:

What kind of work do *I* want to do on a day-to-day basis?

What do *I* want to do
with my leisure time
that would be most meaningful?

What do *I* want to create or build
that would give me
a sense of satisfaction?

The rational consideration of *one's personal experiences and circumstances* is invaluable when reflecting on future goals and life decisions. *The choices that would be in another person's best interest may not be in one's own best interest.* Therefore, for each goal that comes to mind it would be helpful to ask:

What would be the consequences
to *me* if I pursued
this particular goal?

What would *I* gain?

What would *I* lose?

What burden would this choice
place on *my* health, time,
money and relationships?

Is this something
that is in *my* best interest
or is this something
that would be satisfying
only to my parents or my peers?

Rationally pursuing goals also means making life choices for today *and* tomorrow. To be sure, much enjoyment in life can be experienced by focusing on and savoring the present moment.

However, it would be irrational to live only for today. As William Glasser reminds us in his book *Reality Therapy,* the danger in telling ourselves "Eat, drink, and be merry because tomorrow you may die" is that the probability remains that "we will not die tomorrow but instead live on to reap only too fully the negative consequences of short-sighted pleasure seeking." Admittedly, there are many examples of people who postponed the pleasures of the immediate moment only to die before they could reap the full benefits of their long-term planning. Moreover, life would be very difficult to bear if *all* immediate pleasures were postponed for future goals. However, if life is to be filled with deep-seated and lasting satisfaction, it is well to forego *some* of the pleasures of the immediate moment and rationally pursue long-term, greater gains.

Pursuing these long-term goals in a rational way means asking and answering such questions as "Where do I want my life to be in one year?" "In five years?" More specifically, "Where do I want to be in my work next year?" "In five years?" "What do I want my health to be next year?" "In five years?" Since some of our values, interests and preferences gradually change, we would do well to keep asking questions about the things we value month after month and year after year. Initially, we may experience considerable difficulty in identifying long-term goals, but most people experience this. And persistence in asking questions until some answers are found will become easier with time.

It is important to recognize that a goal may be either unrealistic or realistic but meaningless or realistic and meaningful. Someone's goal is unrealistic if it cannot be achieved by anyone with similar ability under similar circumstances, as when a blind man says, "I want to complete college in two years and receive an A in every course." A goal that is possible to achieve but has no defined end points is realistic but meaningless and is characteristic of people who tell themselves, "I want to be better educated," or "I want to be a good secretary." But if a woman who has graduated from college with excellent grades decides, "I want to earn a master's degree in journalism because it is the area in which I have the most interest," she has a realistic and meaningful goal because it is possible to achieve and it has defined end points.

A person who begins to identify some long-term *realistic and meaningful* goals that are desirable would do well to distinguish between what *he* or *she* wants to do in life and what *other people* want him or her to do. Consequently, it is helpful to ask the following questions:

Are these the goals that *I* want
to pursue over the next few years,
or are they goals that my parents,
friends and other people
want me to pursue?

What would be the consequences
to *me* if I pursued this goal or that one
over the next five years?

What would be gained? What would
be lost?

What demands would this goal
or that one place on my health, time,
money and personal relationships?

A person
is constantly
called upon
to create his own future.

**Are these goals in my best interest,
or will they create *unwanted*
economic hardships, emotional upsets
or interpersonal conflicts?**

After several realistic and meaningful long-term goals are identified, it is most advantageous to select and pursue the one that is valued most in order to avoid overtaxing one's physical and psychological resources. Overtaxing on a physical level is a factor in many heart attacks and physical disorders. On a psychological level, it leads to lowered efficiency and, if intense or prolonged, can seriously impair one's ability to think and act in a rational, responsible way. Thus it is well to pursue one long-term goal at a time. Once it is realized, an additional one can be established.

A person who accurately defines the conditions that control the achievement of a realistic and meaningful goal can more easily clarify the direction to take and the strategy to use. If the goal is a specific occupation or profession, it is important to deal with the questions of time, money and special training involved. Until all of these relevant conditions are clarified and defined, a person cannot devise any realistic strategies for achieving the sought-for goal.

The most efficient way to gather information about such conditions is to interview people who are recognized experts in the field. The most obvious sources are institutions, organizations or employers that are directly involved with the goal. The next best source may be a local college or university where one is likely to find at least one professor who teaches a subject related to the goal in question. Community service agencies also have experts who may be able to provide assistance.

Roger Golde, in *Can You Be Sure of Your Experts?*, suggests that if a highly specialized goal is to be pursued, it is wise to consider contacting a magazine editor. Virtually every specialty manages to publish at least one periodical. A listing of these magazines is available in the *Standard Periodical Directory* or *Ulrich's International Periodicals Directory*, which can be found in most public or university libraries. Golde also recommends asking the editor of the particular section of the magazine bearing on the goal (not the editor-in-chief) for the names of experts in the particular area. Specialty editors are engaged primarily in gathering specific kinds of information, and they usually can provide the facts desired.

In preparing to interview a goal expert, it is practical to devise a tentative list of questions so that the specific facts desired will not be forgotten in the course of the conversation. Since the purpose of the interview is to determine each of the conditions involved in achieving the goal and the specific ways which may help to meet these conditions, such questions as the following could be considered:

How much time is required?
What training is needed?
How much money is needed?
What other conditions are involved, e.g., travel, schedules, routines? How would they involve me?

It is recommended that complete notes be taken during the interview. The expert may also be able to identify a useful pamphlet or book that would serve as a handy reference if additional questions come up.

After interviewing the expert, one could ask such questions as the following:

What specific resources do I have?

Do I have the energy, patience and other traits required?

Do I have the financial resources required?

Do I have family members or friends who can help me secure the resources I need?

What specific liability do I have that could interfere with the achievement of my goal, e.g., health problems?

How can I manage my liability so that it does not prevent me from achieving my goal?

The next step is to identify and either reduce or forego the habits and immediate pleasures that place an unnecessary or undue strain on the resources required to effectively pursue the goal. Giving up some immediate pleasures or enjoyable habits is perhaps the major obstacle to the achievement of long-range goals. To be sure, it would be wonderful if we could continue to enjoy all the things that we enjoy now and still achieve the long-range goal that gives lasting satisfaction; but such achievement usually requires some change in daily routines and habits. Thus it is important to identify and either reduce or eliminate the habits and immediate pleasures that are wasting the resources required for a long-term goal.

The important thing is this:

to be able

at any moment

to sacrifice what we are

ecome.

for what we could

Perhaps the three most precious personal resources are health, time and money, and it would be advisable to determine the regulation of one's daily life so that each of these resources is not misused or wasted.

In *How Not To Die Young,* Joan Gomez points out that if you hope to enjoy good health for a reasonable life span, you need to care for your body at least as well as you need to care for your car. "You need to get it inspected periodically and examined for minor faults that might cause trouble later and for signs of wear or damage. For a car it is called servicing; for a human body, screening. Any small abnormalities should be dealt with promptly, even if they don't seem too important in themselves." People will be especially concerned about how their habits affect the top-risk areas of their bodies such as the heart and arteries, the lungs and other vital organs. The implications for their daily life may be to give up smoking, get adequate sleep, exercise regularly, have a balanced diet, give up high-cholesterol foods and keep their weight within normal limits. People will also be concerned about the special pitfalls for themselves as individuals such as careless driving habits and overuse of alcohol and medications. In short, they will recognize that in order to achieve long-term goals, it is essential to keep their heads on their shoulders and their bodies in good operation, and to do both may require some changes in life style.

Time is an irretrievable personal resource. Whenever possible, it is advisable to do one's own scheduling. On the following page there are suggestions on how to best utilize time.

How to best utilize time:

1 Have an appointment book that provides sufficient space to schedule appointments, tasks, deadlines, etc., for each half hour of the day. (An example of a daily time schedule *with special columns* is found on the following page.)
2 Identify the periods of the day that can be set aside for pursuing the goal. If special periods of the day are required, identify them and, where possible, schedule other daily tasks around them.
3 Fill out a time schedule a week in advance.
4 Schedule the tasks to be completed each day in terms of their order of importance.
5 Complete and check off each task and appointment as scheduled.
6 Inventory the schedule at the end of the week in order to determine where most of the time is going and how it can be saved on each task and appointment.
7 Identify and record the distractions—people, activities or events that interfere with the daily schedule.
8 Devise ways of either managing the distractions or modifying the weekly schedule. If important appointments or telephone calls seriously interfere with the schedule, re-group them. Also, plan to take phone calls on a call-back basis and stick to this policy for everything except emergency matters. If possible, have someone else answer the phone and take down the calls that are to be returned.

Daily time schedule

date:

Time	Tasks to be completed	Tasks completed	Appointments	Special deadlines	Distractions to be avoided	Pleasures to be given up
7:00 a.m.						
7:30						
8:00						
8:30						
9:00						
9:30						
10:00						
10:30						
11:00						
11:30						
12:00 noon						
12:30						
etc.						

The purpose of a weekly and daily schedule is to help set aside enough time to pursue the desired goal. Finding enough time may make it necessary to rearrange the schedule, postpone the pursuit of less important goals or delegate responsibility to others for completing time-consuming tasks.

Making optimal use of available money can be done by preparing a budget six months in advance. This requires: a) ordering priorities and determining what is valued most; b) determining how much money it is necessary to earn; c) determining where excess spending on less important goals can be cut; d) gaining the agreement and support of family members who are affected; and e) making a commitment to abide by the self-restraints established. By planning in advance, one can gather valuable information about many of the material and human resources available for pursuing a long-range goal.

After determining how to make the best use of personal resources, plan a strategy that will assure the best chance of goal achievement or at least provide some degree of goal satisfaction. It would be well to keep the following three points in mind: First, there is no way of knowing in advance whether or not the preferred goal will be achieved. Therefore it is advisable to plan a strategy that will not close off other goals in the event of failure to achieve the original one. This will provide an opportunity to achieve success in some other area. Thus a young woman would not summarily abandon her education when she desires to marry but would either postpone marriage or work out an arrangement for combining it with further schooling. Such a strategy would enable her to gain a reasonable degree of satisfaction in at least one important area.

Second, choose a strategy that will permit placing some personal resources in reserve to make possible second and third attempts to achieve the goal if problems are encountered along the way. For example, if a young man wants to begin a business, he would do well to invest a modest portion of his resources. This will not lead to instant wealth, but neither will it lead to bankruptcy. If serious problems arise in certain areas of the business venture, enough resources will be in reserve to make changes that will give it a better chance of succeeding. If the first venture fails, sufficient resources will be available to pursue an alternative venture.

Third, choose a strategy that provides an option whereby a large portion of the invested resources could be transferred into an alternate goal if the original one is not achieved. It is wise for a young man who plans to pursue a career in medicine to give serious consideration to what he would do if—after three or four years in pre-med—he discovers that a medical career was a mistake for him. Could he, and would he want to use his education to pursue a profession not completely alien to medicine—perhaps as a biologist, a laboratory technician, a veterinarian? It is important to remember that *the choices that will be open tomorrow will depend on how wisely plans and choices are made today.*

Consider other possible or probable consequences of using a particular strategy. It may be valuable to ask the question:

> Will this strategy cause
> unwanted personal or interpersonal
> conflict or conflicts that outweigh
> the good that would be achieved?

Each of the following criteria can be used to examine this question:

1 Ethical and legal implications
   (What kind? How serious?)
2 Individuals and/or groups
   affected (Which ones? In what way?)
3 Costs
   (For whom? What kind? How much?)
4 Problems that may be created
   (For whom? What kind? How serious?)

A final point about rational planning is that if people find themselves putting off the task of making a decision, it most likely is because they want to be certain that they are making the wisest decision. However, there are no guaranteed-to-work strategies, only strategies that have a greater or lesser chance of succeeding. Therefore it is advantageous to identify the alternatives and to weigh the advantages and disadvantages of each. Then it is imperative to make a decision and act.

In some instances the alternate courses of action identified may ultimately be unsatisfactory. Yet it is far better to initiate some action when action is warranted than to take none at all.

Unfortunately the latter is what many people do constantly. As a consequence, they gain very little satisfaction in life. The man who constantly avoids committing himself to a graduate program because no program is everything he has envisioned very effectively prevents himself from receiving many possible kinds of satisfaction. No one can be absolutely certain that any one decision will prove to be the wisest. However, indecision is usually far less satisfying than a decision to pursue an imperfect course of action.

Facing problems honestly and responsibly

Life would be simple if projected goals could always be achieved or even achieved with little effort. However this is seldom the case. Problems will be encountered which can temporarily prevent one from achieving the goals. A man may be temporarily or permanently disabled by an accident, may suffer a serious and debilitating physical illness such as a heart condition or kidney ailment. Or he may suffer losses—loss of money and other resources, loss of friendships and loved ones. In addition, someone may encounter changing social and economic conditions which will require making major adjustments in work and family relationships and giving up one role to accept a new one. When problems interfere with goal achievement, it is necessary to accept the problems for what they are and deal with them honestly and responsibly.

Accepting problems for what they are means that a person does not rationalize. Rationalizing is inventing an excuse in order to do what is known to be dishonest or irresponsible, or inventing an excuse in order to avoid doing what is known to be more honest or responsible. The abortion-on-demand proposal may be an example of rationalization for some people. If a woman *believes* that there is a separate human being at the moment of conception but upon learning of her own unwanted pregnancy seeks to avoid personal accountability, she may tell herself that she and she alone shall decide how to control her own reproductive system and that an abortion is in order. To be sure, she has the right to talk to herself and act as she wishes. However, given her original belief, she would be more responsible if she told herself that although she does not like the fact that she is pregnant, people manage human reproduction rationally by finding ways that human life can be protected and cared for when it is unplanned or personally unwanted.

A more common example of rationalizing is found among people who complain that their work is boring and that they wish they could do something else. When asked why they don't, they say that they would have to go back to school or accept a cut in pay, or that all jobs are boring. These answers, of course, are rationalizations. When people tell others, "I would like to do different things but . . . ", they are really telling themselves, "I would like to do different things if I could do so magically without any long-term commitment, work or risks. But since it requires persistent effort, hard work and practice, and since I already can enjoy myself to some degree without this kind of involvement, I don't see why I should try to change." But this is precisely why many people are not dealing effectively with life's complexities and challenges—because they want to do so magically, without any commitment, hard work, or risks. They would do well to accept the fact that there is no short cut or magic in achieving greater satisfaction in life. To get something better they have to commit themselves to a realistic and meaningful goal, work in small but concrete steps each day, and give up the habits and routines of today that interfere with achieving the good that is hoped for tomorrow.

Accepting a problem for what it is means that no one is blamed for disappointments or failures. To be sure, when external events or one's own mistakes interfere with the satisfaction of one's desires, it can be very irritating and frustrating. However, blame, whether of oneself or others, serves no useful purpose. Self-blame leads to anger and depression and, if prolonged, to self-hate; blaming others will lead only to resentment, counter-accusation and bitterness. The realistic satisfaction of personal desires depends on personal willingness to accept a problem for what it is, to avoid blaming oneself or others for being fallible and for living in an imperfect world, and to focus attention and resources on honest ways of solving the problem.

Accepting a problem also means that other escape measures are not resorted to, i.e., alcohol or other drugs. When a problem arises, it is tempting to blot out one's awareness of it with drugs. However, this kind of escape is only temporary; and when the effects of drugs fade, the original situation still remains. Relief is never lasting. Moreover, two problems result: the original one and the new one involving drugs. Eventually people pay for their brief periods of escape, and the costs are usually enormous, possibly with damage to physical health, mental stability and personal relationships.

The search for a satisfactory solution to a problem involves acquiring as much information as possible with regard to workable solutions. Each is then weighed in terms of the individuals that it may affect, the new problems that it may create and the consequences if it fails. If the solution deals with all of the practical and ethical issues involved, this is indeed fortunate. But if a totally satisfactory solution is not possible, it is advisable to choose an ethical course of action that provides the greatest satisfaction. People who are unethical in dealing with their problems are pursuing a course that is fraught with danger. Dishonesty with oneself can begin to erode reason and sanity. The next time a similar situation appears, it will be more difficult to keep from being unethical because previous unethical behavior has already been rationalized.

Finally, people would do well to recognize that if, despite their efforts, things do not turn out well for them and they have tried their utmost to improve their situation, the only rational thing to do is to accept and enjoy the satisfaction that they can get from the responsible course of action they have chosen.

three

Personal relationships

three

A fulfilling relationship, whether with a spouse, parent, child or friend, is an *interdependent* one in which *both* persons identify their wants and adopt behavior patterns that satisfy them in realistic and mutually agreeable ways.

More specifically, a relationship will be fulfilling when both persons:

1 are honest about their own experiences;
2 listen to and understand each other's experiences;
3 identify their realistic wants and identify rational ways of satisfying them;
4 form and honor agreements that enable them to fulfill their wants in mutually satisfying ways;
5 resolve problems and conflicts through mutual agreements.

Being honest

If people can save their lives or prevent physical harm to themselves by being dishonest, then it is rational to be dishonest. One has nothing to lose and everything to gain. However, it is irrational for people to tell themselves that they have everything to gain and nothing to lose by being dishonest in an intimate relationship. In most cases the opposite is true. Yet many people seek a fulfilling relationship through dishonest means. They tell themselves that they cannot be honest because they may hurt the other person. In reality their unwillingness to be honest is based on the fear that they may hurt themselves, that if they are honest, the other person may reject them. However, no one can *make* another person be accepting regardless of the kind of dishonesty used. To be sure, one can use ploys to manipulate, flattery to impress, or threats to intimidate the other for the sake of a positive response. However, sooner or later such behavior will fail to elicit acceptance, trust, love or respect from the other person. The only way to find someone who will demonstrate acceptance, trust, love or respect is to share personal experiences, values and beliefs without reservations and let the other person choose. In this way one has nothing to lose and everything to gain. If such sharing is rejected, one will know immediately that a relationship most likely would not prove satisfying. If there is acceptance, it will demonstrate that it is not necessary to maintain a facade or pretense. Being true to oneself and to the other person and having one's ideas and behavior accepted for what they are will most surely be a satisfying experience.

Listening to and understanding each other

If we want others to listen to and understand *our* wants, we would do well to listen to and understand *their* wants. This means finding the time to listen. If a too-busy signal is heard, the other person may become too-busy as well. Setting aside listening time means being willing to give another person complete attention, to listen to the other person talk about whatever is on his or her mind—work, disappointments, fears, hopes, etc.

Bear in mind that everyone wants to be understood, and understanding comes from accepting what the other person is communicating. In his book *On Becoming a Person,* Carl Rogers suggests that acceptance is shown by listening without criticizing, judging or censoring. Asking questions can insure real understanding. According to Rogers, questions that paraphrase what the other person is communicating are especially helpful. For example, if someone talks to you about being unappreciated, it may be helpful to respond with a question such as "You believe that you have been ignored?" Questions that help people express their thoughts and feelings serve to build understanding. Believing that they are understood, people are more willing to *analyze* their self-talk and behavior.

Identifying realistic wants

For a relationship to be highly rewarding, both persons not only want to be honest in disclosing their experiences and thoughts and active in listening to and understanding each other, but they also want to discover each other's important wants and identify ways of effectively satisfying them. Specifically, both persons would determine: a) what they want most in the relationship;

b) what kinds of interactions would be most effective in helping them to satisfy their wants in constructive ways; and c) whether the consequences of pursuing their wants in the manner that they desire would be in their best interest.

In working to identify their wants and the interactions that would satisfy them, it is important for both persons to make decisions based on the *circumstances of their relationship* and not on the guides and standards of other people. The difficulty with using outside standards is two-fold. First, there are many propagandists who purport to give scientific information but offer only biased opinions which usually reflect their own personal wants. Some sex doctors do a very poor job in helping people set realistic and meaningful sex goals. The so-called facts that they dispense about the kinds of sexual activities that are okay in a relationship are not only often irrelevant (because they are based on other peoples' relationships) but very often misleading. A sex doctor's opinions may suggest to some that if they are opposed to having sex at the time and in the way that the doctor's sex manual advises, they are in some way "hung up." It is important to recognize that the use of outside standards in a relationship, whether the standards be about sexual behavior or anything else, is irrelevant and potentially harmful to a relationship. Outside standards involve somebody else's relationship and somebody else's wants, circumstances and values. *What is rational in one person's relationship may be irrational in another's.* It is most wise, therefore, to be concerned, not with other peoples' relationships or with other peoples' beliefs about what a

35

person needs, but with the particular wants and circumstances in *one's own* relationship.

The second difficulty with using outside standards is that they can be manipulated. As William Lederer and Don Jackson caution in *The Mirages of Marriage,* when outside standards are used, each person tends to quote the standard that most fits his or her own case or gives the greatest advantage. The wife who wants her own car may tell herself and her husband, "We're the only family in the whole block that doesn't have two cars." Or the husband who wants his wife to fix breakfast for him may tell himself and his wife, "I'm the only man in the office whose wife doesn't get up and fix his breakfast." Realistic choices and personal satisfaction cannot be achieved by looking outward at other people's wants, circumstances and values. Only by looking inward at the realities of one's own personal relationship can this be achieved. Whether personal preferences or choices would be acceptable to people outside one's relationship is irrelevant. If they are in the best interest of one's own relationship, it can flourish, and that is what counts.

Forming and honoring mutual agreements

An effective way of having wants satisfied with regularity in a relationship is to agree on and adhere to a set of rules about the roles, schedules, routines, frequencies and other patterns that are desirable on a day-to-day basis.

Forming agreements. The formation of agreements is a joint effort, with decisions arrived at in the absence of compulsion on the part of each person. Each has a right, equal to the other's right, to determine what goes on. Each offers ideas which are sympathetically and responsibly evaluated until both decide on mutually acceptable ones. Using this approach, it is not necessary for one person to persuade the other to accept a particular proposal because both share in the decision making and no one loses.

It is important to emphasize again that both persons would do well to define and agree to rules that make sense to *them*—that are based on *their* wants, values, circumstances, etc. As noted earlier, the difficulty with using outside standards is twofold: First, there are many propagandists who give information or rules which may be realistic or satisfying for other people or for them but which may not be realistic or satisfying for oneself. Second, one can use outside standards selectively to assure one's own way everytime. An honest and responsible decision about the rules for any relationship will be made, not by following guides or fashions that other people choose or propose, but by selecting rules based on *one's own realistic wants and circumstances.* Whether the patterns or rules would be acceptable to people outside of the relationship is irrelevant. Where the rules are legal and ethical, and where they satisfy the realistic wants of both parties and are accepted by them, a relationship can be very fulfilling, and that is what matters.

Honoring agreements. Once mutual agreements about interactions and rules are made, they are

I feel the
capacity to **C**are
is the thing
which gives life
its deepest significance.

to be honored. When an agreement is broken by either person, trouble begins. If a person breaks an agreement, the other may believe that he or she has been betrayed and may try to develop an interpersonal strategy which will protect his or her self-interest. If a wife comes home from a week's visit with her parents and finds that her husband, without previously consulting her, has invited his brother to live with them for a month and that the brother is occupying her newly remodeled sewing room, she may tell herself that she has been betrayed. The sewing room was remodeled for her, and no one else in the family—according to the agreement—was going to use it. Her husband has broken that agreement. How the wife expresses her irritation will depend on the nature of their relationship and on the way she talks to herself about the broken agreement. She may tell herself that he should pay for it. Accordingly, she may insist that new curtains be custom-made for each room, be rude to her husband's brother, complain that no one except her does any work around the house, and start nagging her husband about the budget. Whatever the reaction, she implies that she is having difficulty managing the house because her brother-in-law is in her sewing room and that her husband is responsible for the difficulty. Although she could talk more rationally to herself about her husband's mistake, obviously he was not as sensitive and honest as the agreement with his wife required.

It becomes clear that honesty with oneself and sensitivity to the possible consequences of one's behavior is essential to make an agreement work. Without honesty and sensitivity, no agreement will keep a relationship together. With them, a mutually satisfying agreement will ensure a fulfilling relationship.

Resolving problems

Three kinds of problems can develop in a relationship. The first person may have a grievance against the other; the other may have a grievance against the first or both may share a problem.

Lodging a grievance. If one believes that the other person is not being sufficiently honest, is not listening to one's wants, or is not honoring an agreement, it is advisable to communicate the grievance in a way that encourages the other to respond in a constructive fashion rather than in a defensive or hostile one. George Weinberg suggests, in *The Action Approach,* that there is no set of rules that will guarantee a totally satisfactory response to a grievance. However, some techniques are more likely to elicit constructive responses. Consider the following:

1 State the grievance as soon as it can be articulated. It is the unsaid things that pile up day after day that lead to resentment and bitterness and that gradually destroy a relationship.

2 State the grievance in private to avoid the destructive face-saving and retaliatory behavior that often occurs with public discussion of interpersonal problems.

3 State how pleased you are with many aspects of the other person's behavior before lodging the complaint. It is advisable not to permit a

grievance to overshadow the positive aspects of a relationship.

4 In lodging a grievance use "I don't like" statements such as, "I don't like to be disappointed," instead of "You are" statements such as, "You are inconsiderate." "You are" statements are accusations, and accusations lead only to counter-accusations and emotional upsets.

5 Focus on the *actions* that are unpleasant, not on the other person's possible motives. The fact that someone has done something that is annoying doesn't logically imply that the intention was to cause pain. It may have been. But it may not. In any case, actions not motives are the issue.

6 Do not compare the other person's actions with the failings of other people. The other person is accountable only for personal actions and not for the misdeeds of others.

7 Do not dredge up the past. The present and not the past is the central issue.

8 Focus on one and only one complaint. If more than one grievance is lodged at a time, the other person may believe that he or she is being attacked. The essential issue may then become obscured.

9 Propose, in a non-angry and non-demanding manner, some of the realistic ways that the problem could be satisfactorily resolved.

10 Make every reasonable effort to work out a specific agreement about the way the present problem could be handled.

Receiving a grievance. In the course of a relationship, other people may direct grievances at us. There are no rules that make it easy to receive them. However, as George Weinberg points out, we do not have to upset ourselves "no matter what other people say about us." The following suggestions may be helpful:

1 Put aside whatever is being done when receiving a grievance and look directly at the person talking. Only in this way can sufficient attention be given to what is being said.

2 Listen, and let the other person talk. Everyone wants to be heard. If there are "You are" statements such as, "You are inconsiderate," translate them into appropriate "You don't like" statements, e.g., "You mean you don't like it when you're not consulted?"

3 Accept the grievance as the other person's way of seeing things. However, do not minimize the validity of what is being said. If there are exaggerations, do not make an issue of it.

4 Do not misrepresent the other person's statement. If it is, "You are unfair," do not claim that it means, "You are vicious," and then argue about a charge that was not made.

5 Do not accuse the other person of being irrational, defensive or oversensitive. While the other's behavior is important, it is not the central issue and can be discussed at another time.

6 Do not imply that the other person has some ulterior, hostile or sinister motive for lodging the grievance. *Your behavior,* not the other person's motives, is the issue.

7 Do not laugh at or joke about the grievance nor evade or change the subject. The grievance is as important to the other person as your grievance is to you. Jest, flippancy and

evasions indicate a lack of concern and only add insult to injury.

8 Ask for an opportunity to respond to the grievance after the other person has finished. Indicate that the grievance has been heard. Paraphrase it and ask whether the paraphrase accurately reflects the matter. Describe the information that you had at the time of your decision and explain how you interpreted the information.

9 Defend your actions if you honestly believe that the other person's rights were respected. If it is discovered that they were not, admit it.

Joint problems. In the course of discussing a grievance it may become clear that both persons have a problem. Such problems are inevitable, and one's response to shared problems may be the most critical factor in determining whether a relationship will be healthy or unhealthy, satisfying or unsatisfying. Bear in mind that problems per se do not automatically define how a person responds to them. Each response is determined by the individual's self-talk.

A primary factor in trying to resolve shared problems is for both persons to avoid telling themselves, "I have to win." The "I-have-to-win" attitude creates a power struggle in which each person has the solution to a problem and is trying to persuade or force the other to accept it. Each insists, "I have to have my way and I'm going to get it," and is unconcerned about the wants of the other. When a solution is reached, one goes away feeling angry and, frequently, hostile toward the "winner." However, power is not a responsible or constructive way of solving interpersonal problems. A power solution produces only the illusion of winning for the stronger person. In reality both are losers. There is resentment, strain, and loss of respect.

The alternative to the "I-have-to-win" method is problem solving by mutual agreement, which, as Thomas Gordon points out in *Parent Effectiveness Training,* is commonly used in our society to resolve family and labor-management disputes. Employing this method, both persons participate in a joint search for a solution that will be mutually acceptable. Specifically, the following five steps are used in problem solving by mutual agreement.

1 Identify and define the problem. Each individual explicitly states personal wants. Both avoid blaming the other for the problem.
2 List possible alternative solutions. Each person asks, "What can we do so that I can have what I want and you can have what you want?" Both suggest as many proposals as possible to try to answer this question.
3 Evaluate each proposal according to each person's realistic wants and circumstances and then select the most advantageous solution. Both persons may discover that they *both* cannot have *exactly* what they want. In such instances they would be wise to settle for a solution that will most likely work and help them enjoy a *reasonable degree* of satisfaction.
4 Determine ways of implementing the solution. Spell out *who* is to do *what* at *which time,* i.e., the specific actions, schedules, routines, roles, places, frequencies, and whatever else is in-

volved in implementing the solution that has been selected.

5 Monitor the implementation of the solution and evaluate its effectiveness. This step enables each person to determine whether the solution is producing the desired results. Feedback may reveal that it is adequate. On the other hand, feedback may indicate that it would be better to go back to the drawing board and find a more effective one.

Again, beware of outside standards in searching for and choosing a solution to a personal problem. While many social thinkers are looking for ways of improving on the monogamous marriage, there are many propagandists and self-appointed experts of the new life-style revolution who recommend that we summarily give up the monogamous marriage in favor of communal living, polygamy and other arrangements. The propagandist is looking for a perfect solution to the loneliness that we all feel from time to time. The person seeks an arrangement which will give much and require little and wants the escape option that can be exercised when unpleasant problems arise in relationships. Such an individual wants an arrangement to be a psychedelic jackpot, then discovers that it is not and wants the license to pursue the fantasy with someone else.

Because marriage, like every other kind of arrangement between two separate persons, is often frustrating, limiting and occasionally painful, the propagandist says that marriage is a hopelessly antiquated institution. The steadily increasing divorce rates are presented as evidence. Yet such evidence shows not that the monogamous marriage is a failure but that more and more people are having difficulty both in *choosing a companion* with whom they can share their journey and in *living in communion* with another person. The problem is not with marriage but with the people who are unwilling or unable to be honest and realistic with each other before and during marriage. (For people who want specific advice and procedures for working out their marriage problems, *The Mirages of Marriage* is highly recommended, even over such recent books as *Open Marriage*.)

There is also the myth that the first couple of years of a close relationship are the period during which (1) both persons learn all that they need to know about each other's wants, and (2) all conflicts get resolved. The implications seem to be that thereafter each person's wants do not change and the relationship can roll along productively on its own. This conception is irrational and hazardous. A close relationship, as is most vividly portrayed between husband and wife, is a *process* involving changing wants, and as such it requires both persons to work *continually* on their relationship. Remember that *what is rational and productive in one set of life's circumstances may not be rational and productive in another.* Therefore, both persons would do well to continually monitor their wants, behavior and agreements in order to determine whether their relationship is fulfilling. Where their wants change and where interactions and rules are no longer satisfying, both would seek to discover and implement more satisfying agreements in order to nourish their growing relationship.

four

Accepting ourselves and our world

four

People may become very upset over the disappointments, frustrations, and losses encountered in pursuing goals and in living with others and may believe that their unpleasant experiences are the direct cause of their unhappiness. They may think that when they fail to succeed at something and become depressed, their failure is the direct cause of their depression. They may also feel that when they are mistreated by someone else and become hostile, the mistreatment is the direct cause of their hostility. Further, they may believe that when they suffer a loss and become hysterical, their loss is the direct cause of their hysteria. It seems logical to conclude that one's unpleasant experiences make one upset and unhappy. However, it will be recalled from Chapter 1 that:

> **It is not the experiences people have but the thoughts they tell themselves that determine**
> **how they feel and act.**
> **People make themselves upset and unhappy by talking to themselves in irrational ways.**

In *A Guide to Rational Living,* Albert Ellis brilliantly articulates many of the irrational statements that unhappy people continually tell themselves. In my judgment, nearly all emotional upsets and periods of unhappiness are created by two irrational thoughts that people tell themselves:

1 **I should always perform perfectly, and if I fail to do so, I am a worthless person.**
2 **People and life should always treat me in a totally satisfying way, and if they fail to do so, they are awful and unbearable.**

Accepting ourselves as fallible human beings

As children, many of us were told by parents, teachers, church officials and others that we should perform in a totally competent and responsible way; and if we failed to do so, we were no good. Unthinkingly, we made this irrational idea a basic part of our self-talk repertoire. As a result, practically every time we perform, we don't say, "I would *like* to perform *well*," but we tell ourselves, "I *should* perform *perfectly.*" Some examples of "I should perform" self-talk:
1 I should get all A's.
2 I should get an executive position with a prestigious company.
3 I should be a perfect spouse and perfect parent.
4 I should be a perfect administrator.

49

People tell themselves that they should perform perfectly because it is believed that *imperfection signifies worthlessness.* Some examples of such self-talk:

1 If I don't get all A's, I'm a failure (and worthless).
2 If I don't get an executive position with a prestigious company, I'm a nobody (and worthless).
3 If I'm not a perfect spouse and perfect parent, I'm no good.
4 If I'm not a perfect administrator, I'm a terrible person.

From their irrational culture people have learned to believe that they should always perform in a perfect way, and that if they fail to do so, they are worthless. As a consequence, people tell themselves each day that they *have* to succeed (perfectly) in education, business, love and everything else in order to avoid being worthless.

But where is the evidence that a person *should* perform perfectly all of the time or even most of the time? To say, "I *want* to perform competently, and I *want* to act in acceptable ways" is quite rational, but to say, "I *should* always perform in a totally competent and acceptable way," is to demand godlike behavior. But where is the evidence that a human being can achieve perfection or be a god? Is it not true that all of us were created with physical and intellectual limitations and flaws and that there is nothing that we or anyone can do to change this reality? Is it not true that while we would be better off if we didn't make mistakes, *we are fallible human beings who cannot avoid making mistakes?* Then is it not irrational to expect, or be expected by others, to perform perfectly?

Let us assume for a moment that a person could perform perfectly. Is there any reason why he or she *needs* to perform perfectly? For example, does someone really need to perform perfectly in college, in work, or in marriage? Will one collapse and disintegrate upon failing to get all A's and B's in college or not being the most efficient employee or the perfect spouse? Keep in mind that *needs are physical, and they must be met to insure survival, safety and adequate health; but wants are psychological. Survival, safety, health and the ability to give meaning and satisfaction to one's life are not compromised if one's wants are not satisfied.* To be sure, it is advisable to make every reasonable effort to perform as well as possible. The consequences of being incompetent, unethical and rejected are often very unpleasant. So it is in a person's best interest to act in competent, moral, and acceptable ways. However, in order to avoid emotional upsets and periods of unhappiness, one would do well to give up the idea that anyone *should* achieve the impossible, namely, be a "perfect person."

And where is the evidence that limitations, imperfections or mistakes make one a failure, a nobody or worthless? Admittedly, personal behavior can be judged as good or bad in accordance with the goal of living a rational life. That is, if an individual's behavior leads to a productive and relatively conflict-free life, the behavior is good. On the other hand, if a person's behavior prevents the achievement of goals and creates conflicts, the behavior is bad. But good

verybody's got
something
to sing about.

or bad behavior cannot transform one into a good or bad person. While an individual produces behavior, one does not *become* the behavior. Barking like a dog or quacking like a duck does not make one a dog or a duck. Likewise, making a mistake does not make one a mistake. Limitations, imperfections and failures may make a person's life unpleasant, but they can never make one a failure or a worthless person. *Each individual is a fallible human being whose performance cannot change this reality one iota.*

Similarly, the superior competencies, ethics or personal traits of *other people* cannot make a person inferior. One may believe that the talented writer or singer or molder of clay is a "better" person. But such an artisan is only better at *doing* certain things and not at *being* a person. One may believe that someone who acts more considerately is a "better" person; but such an individual is only better at behaving considerately. Regardless of how imperfect the performance in comparison with another person's, one can never become less than a person and can never be "worse" than any other person. *Individuals are all equal as persons because each is a fallible human being—no more and no less—and this reality can never be altered by personal performances or by the performance of others.*

An equally important fact is that other people's negative evaluations of competencies, ethics, or personal traits can never make one no good. When parents call one a failure because of an F grade or when the boss angrily criticizes poor work, one may judge oneself to be no good. But the evidence is that neither parents, nor bosses, nor anyone else can ever *make anyone* less than a fallible human being. Regardless of the judgments that people make, no one can ever be a failure, a nobody or a worthless person. Granted, it is always in one's best interest to rate personal competencies, ethics and traits as either constructive or destructive and to weigh other people's judgments of one's behavior. It is necessary to evaluate behavior in order to improve it. However, one does not want to confuse any part of personal behavior with oneself as a person. While it is advantageous to rate behavior because it is improvable, it is irrational to rate oneself or anyone else because no one can ever be a "better" or "worse" person, only a fallible human being.

People who tell themselves that they are fallible human beings who can never be rated as good or bad persons regardless of their performances and regardless of other people's opinions of them will not be afraid of failure. Nor will they pressure themselves to perform perfectly. Consequently, they will be largely free of anxiety, make fewer mistakes, and be unashamed to acknowledge their failings. On the other hand, people who tell themselves that they can be rated as good or bad persons will be afraid of failure and will continually pressure themselves to perform perfectly. Consequently, they will be highly anxious, make many mistakes, be ashamed of their failings and be inclined to lie, cheat and do whatever else they believe is necessary to cover up their limitations and imperfections. Clearly, if people want to avoid periods of unhappiness and if they want to increase their chances of achieving goals and experiencing fulfilling personal relationships, it is essential that they accept themselves as fallible human beings, refuse to rate themselves as persons, and refuse to interpret the judgments of another as ratings of themselves as persons.

Accepting other people and life

As children, many individuals also learned to tell themselves that people and life should always be pleasing; and if they are not, they are awful and unbearable. As adults, many tell themselves this irrational idea everytime they have an unpleasant experience. They don't say, "I would *like* to be treated *reasonably well* by people and life," but tell themselves, "I *should* be treated *in a totally satisfying way.*" This "I should be treated" self-talk includes:

1 I should always be accepted and respected by my co-workers.
2 I should have a job that is always enjoyable and rewarding.
3 I should be promoted for doing good work.
4 My boyfriend should always keep his promises.

People tell themselves that they should be treated in a totally satisfying way because they believe that disappointments and frustrations signify awful treatment and unbearable suffering. They say to themselves:

1 If my co-workers don't support my proposal, they are bastards.
2 When I work the evening shift, my job is unbearable.

3 If my boss doesn't promote me, he is discriminating against me.
4 If my boyfriend doesn't keep his promise, he is a creep.

From their irrational culture people have learned to believe that they should be treated in a totally satisfying way by others and by life. If they are not, people and life are horrible and unbearable.

But where is the evidence that people and life *should* treat anyone in a perfectly enjoyable way? To say, "I *want* people and events to treat me in a satisfying way," is quite rational; but to say, "I *should* always be treated in a totally enjoyable way," is to demand that others act and events unfold according to one's private wishes. But where is the evidence that these wishes should be given special consideration? One may tell oneself that special treatment should be accorded because of special gifts, because of honesty and kindness, or because of a particular nationality, religion, or color, or because of wealth, status, titles and power. However, neither fortunes nor virtues make one a special person who *should* be treated in a special way. No one is entitled to less work, pain and suffering and more leisure, comfort and enjoyment than anyone else.

Nor is there any evidence that a person *can* be treated in a totally satisfying way by people or life. *All people* are fallible human beings and predisposed to acting thoughtlessly, selfishly and cruelly. Therefore, is it not irrational to expect people to treat us in any way except an imperfect way? *Everything in life* is imperfect and limited. Nothing completely satisfies or lasts. Achievements such as wealth, position, power, honor, fame, cannot satisfy the desire for knowledge or love or justice. Nor are achievements permanent. They are controlled by circumstances, and they must all be left at death. Nor do gifts such as beauty and strength satisfy or last. The shadows of disease, accident, age and death are flung over them all.

The pursuit of knowledge, while essential to a productive and rewarding life, cannot give total answers in the longest life-time and is always limited. The pursuit of knowledge can disappoint by revealing more of the unknown, the inaccessible and the contradictory. Virtue demands continuous self-control and self-denial, and nothing difficult can completely satisfy since one would be more satisfied if one could be virtuous without difficulty.

Neither can pleasure totally satisfy or last. Pleasure is simply a brief experience that accompanies the use of one's capabilities, and no capability can be exercised without eventually producing fatigue, pain and dissatisfaction.

It is an illusion to believe that wealth, knowledge, virtue, pleasure or anything else in life can ever satisfy all of one's wants. Each has its purpose, and each has its limitations. Money can satisfy only money-wants, knowledge only the desire for knowledge, sex only sex-wants. If everything in life is limited and imperfect, is it not irrational to *expect* life to treat one in a totally satisfying way?

Assume for a moment that people and life *could* treat one perfectly; is there any reason why a person *needs* to be treated thus? Does a husband *need* to have sex with his wife everytime he wants it, or even most of the time, in or-

57

The main thing

in life

is <u>not</u> to be afraid

 to be

uman.

der to give meaning to his marriage? Do people *need* to have all co-workers, or even most, like or agree with them in order to pursue personal interests and do creative and satisfying things? To be sure, it is to their advantage to make every reasonable effort to secure the things that are important to them and to have their reasonable rights respected; but human beings do not *need* to have all or even most things *their way* in order to live reasonably happy lives.

Where is the evidence that disappointments, frustrations, or losses are awful and unbearable? Most unpleasant experiences do not truly prevent one from achieving projected goals or from enjoying fulfilling relationships. People interpret experiences as awful because they tell themselves that they *should not* be frustrated or disappointed. Once they accept their unpleasant experiences, they discover that such experiences are rarely catastrophic. Reality may prevent them from achieving certain goals or having certain experiences, but it cannot defeat them or make their lives unbearable. Only the *individual* can make life unbearable by demanding that *things not be the way they are.* As long as life lasts, one can create a meaningful future for oneself because it is always possible to find someone or something in life to live and work for and enjoy.

Viktor Frankl reasserts this truth in his book *Man's Search for Meaning.* In his death camp experience during World War II, Frankl saw many things happening to his fellow prisoners— torture, incineration, shooting and gassing. He saw loyalties and faith dissolve, but most of all he saw despair. However, Frankl discovered that

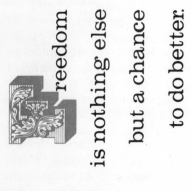

Freedom
is nothing else
but a chance
to do better.

although every scrap of personal property had been taken, although the Nazis were able to strip the body bare and subject it to all kinds of mistreatment, no SS guard or barbed wire could prevent him from believing in his future. For Frankl there was no despair because he had found something that was worth all the suffering that he was experiencing.

Frankl, in turn, helped hundreds of prisoners find something to live and suffer for. He helped them to visualize their wives, sweethearts, children, recall the happy moments they once experienced, and believe that they would again experience such happy moments. It was this belief that *something in the future was worth the pain of the present* that actually pulled Frankl and hundreds of prisoners through the darkness that seemed to have no ending. It was this that enabled them to survive and give meaning to a horrifying experience. Frankl reminds his readers that people can give meaning to any situation if they *resign themselves to the unpleasantness that they encounter and if they choose someone or something to live and suffer for.* "He who has a *why* to live, can bear with almost any *how.*"

In conclusion, when people become unhappy it is usually because they are *grandiose and perfectionistic*—demanding that things be the way they want them to be instead of accepting them as they are. People demand perfect performances from themselves and totally satisfying treatment from others and from life. When individuals fail to meet the perfectionistic demands that they make on themselves, they blame and damn themselves and make themselves upset and unhappy. When other people and life fail to meet the perfectionistic demands, these same individuals blame and damn them, and again make themselves upset and unhappy. As Albert Ellis points out, the pursuit of perfectionism is sheer folly.

> Perfectionism is, almost by definition, a self-defeating philosophy. No matter how close you may come to running the perfect race, living with someone who displays flawless behavior, or arranging things in your life so that you are absolutely certain of their outcome, you will never really achieve your perfectionist goals. For humans are *not* angels; events are *never* certain; decisions *cannot* be absolutely correct at all times. Even if you temporarily achieve perfection in some goal, your chances of remaining at this ultimate peak are nil. Nothing is perfectly static; life *is* change. Whether you like it or not, you'd better accept reality the way it is: as being highly imperfect and filled with most fallible humans. The main alternative is continual anxiety and desperate disappointment.

The message is clear. In order to avoid prolonged unhappiness and in order to give meaning and satisfaction to their brief journey through life, it is essential that persons begin now to stop all of their grandiose and perfectionistic demanding, accept themselves and their world unconditionally, and strive to live as enjoyably and responsibly as they can under the conditions in which they find themselves.

five

Rational
self-counseling

five

People will learn to accept themselves and their world unconditionally and live as enjoyably and responsibly as they can by learning rational self-counseling. This means that they systematically identify, clarify and eliminate the various *irrational* ideas which they tell themselves. This self-counseling process has four steps:

1 Identifying the situation
  that one finds unpleasant.

2 Listing the ideas
  that one is telling oneself
  about the situation.
  a) the awful things
  that it signifies
  b) the things
  that should happen

3 Challenging the self-talk
  in terms of the facts
  about oneself and one's world

4 Working to improve
  what can be improved
  and accepting what cannot.

1 Stating the unpleasant situation

The unpleasant situation that people upset themselves about may involve their imperfections and mistakes, someone else's behavior, or an unfortunate set of circumstances. The situation can be identified by asking and answering such questions as:

1 Have I upset myself over my imperfections and mistakes?
   a) I failed a course.
   b) I make several errors at the office each day.
2 Have I upset myself over another person's behavior?
   a) My boss criticizes my work and insults me.
   b) My boyfriend left me for someone else.
3 Have I upset myself over an unfortunate set of circumstances?
   a) My job is frustrating.
   b) I became partially crippled in an automobile accident.

2 Listing self-talk

Having identified the situation, one lists the things one is telling oneself about the problem. The two important categories of self-talk are (1) the awful things that the situation signifies and (2) the things that should happen.

a *The awful things that the situation signifies*

1) What am I telling myself about my mistakes and failures?
   a) I've ruined my chances for graduate school. People must think I'm a complete idiot. I'll never succeed at anything.
   b) I'm an incompetent secretary. I must be naturally inefficient. I'm so worthless.

65

Be patient
toward all that is unsolved
in your heart
and try
to love the **Q**uestions
themselves.

2) What am I telling myself about my unpleasant experiences with others?

a) My boss is a horrible person. I am always being criticized and insulted. He makes me angry all day long.

b) I must be a worthless person if my boyfriend doesn't want to be with me anymore. I'll never be accepted and loved by anyone.

3) What am I telling myself about my unfortunate life situation?

a) My job is so meaningless, I can't stand it.

b) My life is so horrible as a cripple. I'll never be able to have any enjoyment in life.

b The things that should happen

1) What am I telling myself about the way I *should* perform?

a) I should get A's or B's in all of my courses, especially the courses in my major.

b) I should be as fast at typing, taking shorthand and filing written materials as other secretaries.

2) What am I telling myself about the way people *should* treat me?

a) My boss should always approve of my ideas and work, and he should always be courteous to me.

b) My boyfriend should like *me* and *only* me.

3) What am I telling myself about the way life *should* treat me?

a) I should have a job that has the right hours, money and satisfaction.

b) I should be able to do all the things that other people do.

3 Challenging self-talk

After listing the things that one is telling one-self, a person disputes the irrational self-talk by asking for evidence that the situation signifies awful things or that certain things should happen.

Continuing with the same examples, self-talk could be challenged by asking and answering such questions as the following:

1a (Student who failed a course.)

What rational basis do I have for telling myself that my chances of going to graduate school are ruined? How can the failing of *one* course prevent me from being admitted to graduate school?

Where is the evidence that people think I am a complete idiot? How can I read other peoples' minds to know what they are thinking? Why wouldn't people think I'm simply a fallible human being like everyone else?

What rational basis do I have for telling myself that I'll *never* succeed at *anything?* I succeeded in graduating from high school, and I succeeded in passing several college courses. That proves that I *can* succeed at *some* things.

Where is the evidence that I *should* get A's and B's in all my courses. Since I'm a fallible human being, isn't it illogical to *expect* to be a perfect student?

1b (Secretary who makes several errors.)

What rational basis do I have for telling myself that I am an incompetent secretary? Most of the time I do *not* make typing, shorthand or filing mistakes. If I were incompetent, I would be making mistakes *every second*. I'm simply a fallible human being.

Where is the evidence that I am *naturally* inefficient? "Natural" simply refers to what I have *learned* to do habitually, and *I can learn to make fewer mistakes.*

What rational basis do I have for telling myself that I am worthless when the fact is that I can never be rated as a person, and I can never be less than a fallible human being?

Where is the evidence that I *should* perform secretarial tasks as well as other people? (Even though each of us is a fallible human being, each of us is different with respect to gifts and capabilities.)

2a (Employee who is criticized by boss.)

What rational basis do I have for telling myself that my boss is a horrible person? Isn't he just a fallible human being who does things I don't like? Doesn't practically everyone do things that someone doesn't like?

Where is the evidence that I am always being criticized and insulted? To say that I am *always* criticized and insulted means that *every second* critical and insulting remarks are directed at me. This isn't true.

What rational basis do I have for telling myself that *he* makes me angry all day long? I make myself angry, because I'm telling myself that his words *make me* worthless. But nobody's words can make me less than a fallible human being.

We **A**chieve
according
to what
we **B**elieve.

Where is the evidence that he *should* approve of
my ideas and be courteous? For now, he should
do exactly what he has learned to do—be critical
and insulting.

2b (Girl who was rejected by boyfriend.)

What rational basis do I have for telling myself
that I am a worthless person because my
boyfriend rejected me? If no one can ever make
me less than a fallible person, how can anyone's
rejection of me make me worthless?

Where is the evidence that I'll never be accepted
and loved by anyone? If I lost *one* boyfriend, is
that proof that I'll *never* find *anyone* who will
accept me and love me? Moreover, do I really
need a boyfriend to enjoy life? While I would like
to have one, aren't there many enjoyable things
to do that do not require a boyfriend?

Where is the evidence that my boyfriend
shouldn't have left me for someone else? Since
other people are concerned with their wants more
than with mine and since we made no agreement
to love only each other, why *shouldn't* my
boyfriend pursue his interests with whomever he
wishes? Even if we did have an agreement, why
shouldn't he make mistakes? Isn't he fallible?

3a (Employee who has frustrating job.)

What rational basis do I have for telling myself
that my job is so meaningless? Since *I* give
meaning to things and I can give any meaning I
wish to my work, how can I say it is meaning*less*?

Where is the evidence that I can't stand my job?
It isn't true that I can't stand my work. I already
have stood it. What I mean is that I don't enjoy

my work very much and that I would prefer to do something else.

Where is the evidence that I *should* have a job that has the right hours, money and satisfaction? I'm not a special person who should be treated in a special way. Moreover, practically every job has something imperfect about it, and I would be misleading myself if I believed I could find the perfect job.

3b (Person who became partially crippled.)

What rational basis do I have for telling myself that I am a worthless cripple? If no situation or life condition can ever make me less than a person, how can my unpleasant handicap make me worthless?

Where is the evidence that I'll never be able to have an enjoyable life? Since I can always choose something or someone to live and work for and since I can always do something satisfying under the conditions in which I find myself, I have no rational basis for telling myself that I will *never* be able to have an enjoyable life.

Where is the evidence that I *should* have the things that other people have? Since all of reality is ordered in terms of cause and effect relationships and since the conditions for having an automobile accident and for becoming partially crippled were met, why shouldn't I be handicapped? If I am handicapped, why should I be able to do all the things non-handicapped people can do? It doesn't make any sense to demand that reality be the way I wish it were instead of the way it is.

4 Improving what can be improved

Having challenged both the awful things that the situation signifies and the things that should happen, one rationally plans and implements a course of action that will improve one's life situation, telling oneself the specific courses of action that are possible to take, and then choosing the most advantageous option. Continuing with the same examples, one could talk to oneself in the following way about realistic courses of action:

1a

Since I have failed a course in my major and since it is to my advantage to pass this course, I will take the course again and try to get at least a C in it. I will set aside two hours each day to complete the requirements of this course, and I will get someone to tutor me and help me with my papers. If I fail the course again, TOO BAD! I can and will have a meaningful and satisfying college experience even though I failed a course.

1b

Since I am not as efficient in my secretarial tasks as I would like to be and since I risk losing my job if I am not reasonably efficient, I will complete the training needed to improve my typing, shorthand and filing skills. If I cannot improve my skills as much as I prefer—TOUGH! I can and will live a productive and enjoyable life with the skills I have.

2a

Since I am being criticized and insulted by my boss and since it is to my advantage to have my reasonable rights respected, I will work as calmly and rationally as I can to persuade him not to treat me in an unpleasant way. If I cannot

73

persuade him to treat me in a more satisfying way—THAT'S LIFE! I can and will continue to enjoy satisfying relationships with several of my co-workers.

2b

Since I was rejected by my boyfriend and there is no chance of reconciliation, I will date other boys and try to have the kind of relationship that I prefer. If I cannot find a boy who has all the traits that I like—TOO BAD! I will live as enjoyably as I can with the most desirable boys that I can date.

3a

Since I have a job that is often frustrating and since I would enjoy life more if I did not have such a frustrating job, I will try to find a more pleasant job or retrain to secure a more satisfying position. If I cannot find or secure a better job—TOUGH! I will get as much enjoyment as I can out of my present job.

3b

Since I have become crippled and there is nothing that I can do to change this reality, I will try to develop my talents as best I can. If I cannot do all of the things I would like to do—THAT'S LIFE! I will become absorbed in doing the things that I can do and that give me the greatest satisfaction.

In conclusion, everyone will experience disappointments, frustrations and losses. One will create a meaningful and rewarding life only when one accepts oneself and one's unpleasant experiences unconditionally, recognizes that wants are not needs, works to improve what can be improved, and lives as enjoyably and as responsibly as possible under the conditions that cannot be changed.

Practicing
rational
self-counseling

six

It takes practice and persistence to identify, clarify and eliminate the irrational self-talk that prevents one from fully accepting oneself and one's world and creating and enjoying a meaningful life. Perhaps rational self-counseling is most helpful and rewarding when used for each of the following:
1 eliminating emotional upsets as they occur
2 analyzing past conflicts
3 formulating a more realistic philosophy of life
4 conquering irrational fears
5 helping a companion solve a problem

Eliminating emotional upsets

Successfully eliminating emotional upsets when and as they occur involves applying the four steps of rational self-counseling described in the preceding chapter. On pages 82–83 is a worksheet format utilizing the RSC steps. This format can be used everytime one makes oneself anxious, angry, depressed or otherwise unhappy. (See appendix a for an additional RSC worksheet.)

Analyzing
past conflicts

The purpose of using rational self-counseling to analyze past conflicts is to identify, clarify, and eliminate habitual patterns of self-talk that produce anxiety, depression, or hostility.

When practicing rational self-counseling on a past conflict, one does each of the following as honestly and accurately as possible:

1 Visualize the conflict situation as it existed in the past, i.e., the events, the people and the interactions.

2 Recreate the self-talk that probably went on.

3 Challenge it.

4 Imagine that the past problem has returned and respond to it a second time and in a rational way.

Practicing rational self-counseling on a past problem can help one deal more realistically with future disappointments. Two weeks ago George learned of an executive position that offered him more money than his present job. In applying for the position, he was asked to attend an interview at 4:30 p.m. the next day. He told himself, "I gotta get that job, that's for me;" and "I can't miss that interview." The next day George agreed with his wife, Carol, that since she needed the family car during the day, she would drop him off at work that morning, pick him up promptly at 4 p.m., and drive him to his 4:30 p.m. interview. Since that day was also Carol's birthday, George and Carol planned to go out to dinner after the interview. When 4 p.m. arrived, George said to himself, "Well, I better get going. Carol is waiting for me outside." However, Carol was not waiting outside. George said to himself, "Well, she'll be here any second now." As the minutes ticked away, George became annoyed, saying to himself, "Oh nuts, where is she? Can't she tell time?" At 4:15 George called his home, but there was no answer. "Damn it," George said to himself. "She's supposed to be here at 4 o'clock and not one minute later." As time marched on, George said, "This is awful. She's ruining everything." At 4:30 George called Mr. Jackson, the employer with whom he was to have the interview, and explained his situation. George learned that since he could not attend the arranged interview, he could not be included in the final list of candidates for the new job. It was now after 4:30, and George said, "That goddamn woman really did it to me. She's always messing up my life. Well, we will see about this." George took a bus home, and en route he told himself, "If she doesn't care about me, I don't have to care about her. She wants to go to dinner. Well, I have a surprise for her. We're staying home, and we'll see how she likes it." George arrived home at 5:10 p.m. His wife had also returned, and George confronted her in the kitchen, shouting, "You were supposed to pick me up at 4 o'clock. Where the hell were you? You've ruined everything. Why did you do this to me?" Carol responded, "George, I'm sorry, but I had a flat tire on the expressway and I couldn't get anyone to help me until after 4:30. Did you call Mr. Jackson and explain what happened?" George said, "I don't like being treated like this. Nobody cares about me, so why should I care about other people. I'm not going out to dinner tonight." George left the kitchen, went into the bedroom, and slammed the door.

That was the situation two weeks ago. Today George analyzes the conflict in order to learn how he can respond rationally to this kind of situation in the future. He first visualizes the conflict situation as it existed two weeks ago. Then he recalls the things that he told himself, and he challenges his self-talk. George recalls that he told himself that *he had to get* the higher paying position and that he *couldn't miss* the scheduled interview. A few minutes after 4 p.m. on the day of the interview, he recalls that he told himself, "Carol is supposed to be here at 4 o'clock and not one minute later." George then asks himself, "Where is the evidence that I *had* to get the job or that I *couldn't* miss the interview or that Carol *was supposed* to pick me up? George recognizes that he not only *wanted* things to be a certain way but he *demanded* that they be a certain way.

George next recalls that he told himself, "This is awful. She's ruining everything." He again asks himself, "Where is the evidence that it was *awful* or that everything was ruined?" George recognizes that he *exaggerated the significance of the disappointment.* He also recognizes that *his self-talk,* not Carol or anything else, made him upset.

Finally, George recalls that he told himself, "If she doesn't care about me, I don't have to care about her." He also remembers that he wanted to punish Carol for "mistreating" him; and again he asks himself, "Where is the evidence that I was deliberately mistreated by Carol, and where is the evidence that if I am disappointed, I should punish someone for it?"

ecision
is the alternative
to fear.

George revises his beliefs about his unpleasant experience and pictures himself facing the disappointment a second time and responding calmly and rationally to it. He tells himself, "I wish I had been able to get the better paying job, but there is no reason why I should have gotten the job. It would be to my advantage to have a better paying job; but I'm not awful, and my life is not awful because I didn't get the job. I can and will do many productive and satisfying things in my present job." He also assures himself, "If I have another opportunity to get a better paying job, I will do my best to get it, but I will not *expect* to get it nor will I *demand* that I not be disappointed. I'll accept what happens because I know that even if I don't have things my way, I'm not a failure or a worthless person; and I can always do productive and satisfying things with my life situation."

Formulating a more realistic philosophy of life

As young children growing up, people did not have the level of maturity required to form rational beliefs about everything that was experienced. Consequently, they learned some self-defeating beliefs about themselves and their world and developed some self-defeating responses to life's complexities. These unrealistic beliefs and ways of acting generally persist into adulthood and tend to impede efforts to respond rationally and constructively to each new situation that is encountered.

Possible rational self-counseling worksheet

1 Unpleasant situation

My behavior; other people's behavior; unfortunate circumstances
Example: My boss refused to give me a promotion.

2 Self-talk

A. The awful things my situation signifies

1 My boss thinks I'm incompetent.

2 He is discriminating against me.

3 That bastard didn't promote me because he is punishing me for being outspoken.

3 Rational challenges

Challenging my opinion of situation
Is my opinion true?

Challenging my self-talk

(Is my self-talk true? Where is the evidence? What am I exaggerating? What grandiose or perfectionistic demands am I making? What kind of self-talk will best help me understand my situation and eliminate emotional upsets and interpersonal conflicts?)

part A

1 This is mind reading. I have no way of knowing what my boss thinks about me. If he really does think I'm incompetent, why haven't I been fired? If I believe that others think about me in a certain way is it because *I* think that way about myself? Am *I* the one who thinks I'm incompetent? If so, where is the evidence that I'm incompetent? I am competent enough to do my present job!
2 There are many possible explanations for each person's behavior including my boss. It is irrational to assume that the only explanation is that he is against me.
3 My boss is obviously not the label I put on him. He is simply a fallible human being who fails to do what I would like him to do. How does this kind of self-talk help me do productive things? I'm simply making myself angrier when I use such labels. I don't know why he didn't promote me, and I would do well to find out. Mind reading serves no useful purpose.

4 I'll never get anywhere in this job.

4 This is untrue. The words "never" and "anywhere" are exaggerations. I have specific tasks and I do complete them, so I am very productive. If I mean by these words that I do not always get what I want and hope for in life, that's true. That's the way things are in an imperfect world. I cannot always have things my way.

B. The things that should happen

part B

1 There is no good reason why I shouldn't be promoted.

1 The fact is that there are many reasons why I would not be promoted that have nothing to do with me as a person. For example, nobody promised me a promotion in writing. Am I not demanding a promotion because I believe I *need* one? Don't I believe that I am a *worse* person without one and that I would be a *better* person with one? If so, isn't it a fact that nothing can make me a *worse* or *better* person? And while I desire a promotion, isn't it true that I don't need to be promoted in order to do productive things and enjoy life?

2 That SOB shouldn't be my boss.

2 How does this kind of self-talk help me do productive things? Nonsense labeling serves no useful purpose. My boss should be exactly what he is, an F.H.B. (a fallible human being) who happens to be my supervisor.

4 Rational action strategy

(What kind of strategy will best help me improve the things that can be improved in my situation and accept the things that cannot?)

Since I want a promotion very much, I will ask my boss what the requirements are for receiving one. I will calmly work as diligently and efficiently as is reasonable in order to secure a promotion. If I don't succeed in getting one, I'll accept the outcome and work as enjoyably as I can in my present position.

Below are several sets of questions that may help to:

1 identify some of the irrational beliefs that may have been formed as a child and may continue to be held as an adult;

2 challenge each belief by examining the facts about oneself and one's life; and

3 identify more realistic ways of responding to the events and circumstances in life.

While asking each set of questions, try focusing on all of the thoughts that come to mind in order to examine them as fully as possible. To discover and eliminate irrational beliefs that may be controlling or conditioning one's actions, it is essential to become fully aware of one's thoughts and to write them down as soon as they occur.

1 As a child, did I interpret my parents' behavior to mean that I was a source of enjoyment to them, that I was wanted, accepted and loved? Or did I interpret their behavior to mean that I was a burden to them, that I was unwanted, rejected and unloved?

a) What evidence did I have that my interpretation of my parents' behavior was accurate?

b) What do I tell myself today about *needing* to be accepted and loved? Do I tell myself that I am not accepted and loved enough—that I am not accepted and loved by as many people as I need and in the way that I need? Do I tell myself that I should be accepted and loved in a special way?

c) Why do I believe that I *must* or *should* be accepted and loved in the way I have stated above? Do I believe that I am no good or that my life is unbearable when I am not accepted and loved in the way I want?

d) *Where is the evidence that:* I *must* or *should* be accepted and loved in the way that I want? I *should* be or can be loved in a special way? I am no good, or my life is awful and unbearable when I am not accepted and loved in the way that I want?

e) What would be a realistic belief to hold about myself and my life in view of the fact that I cannot and need not be accepted and loved by as many people as I would like and to the degree that I would prefer?

f) How can I begin to act today toward my spouse, children, friends, peers and co-workers so that I can enjoy life and give meaning to it despite the limited acceptance and love that I receive?

2 As a child, did I interpret my parents' behavior to mean that I was competent, that I could do things well, and that I could achieve personally meaningful goals? Or did I interpret their behavior to mean that I was incompetent, that I could not do anything right, and that I would never amount to much?

a) What evidence did I have that my interpretation of my parents' behavior was accurate?

b) What do I tell myself today about *needing* to be competent? For example, do I tell myself that I am not competent *enough,* that I *should* be totally competent in everything that I do or that I need to be at least as competent as other people? Do I tell myself that I *should be a special person* or that I *should* be *better* than other people?

c) Why do I believe that I *must* or *should* be competent in the ways I have stated above? Do I believe that I am no good or that my life is unbearable when I am not a *better person* or when I do not do all things perfectly?

d) *Where is the evidence that:* I *must* or *should* be competent in the way I want? I should be or can be a special person? I am no good, or my life is horrible and unbearable when I am not totally competent, or when I am not more competent than other people?

e) What would be a realistic belief to hold about myself and my life in view of the fact that I, like everyone else, can not and need not do all or even most things perfectly?

f) How can I begin to act today at work and with my family so that I can enjoy life and give meaning to it with the competencies that I have?

3 As a child, did I interpret my parents' behavior to mean that because people are imperfect and fallible, they will disappoint me, criticize me, frustrate me or reject me, and that it is irrational to blame or punish people for behaving imperfectly toward me? Or did I interpret my parents' behavior to mean that people must not treat me unsatisfactorily and that when people do disappoint me, criticize me, frustrate me, or reject me, they should be punished?

a) What evidence did I have that my interpretation of my parents' behavior was accurate?

b) What do I tell myself today about needing to be treated well by other people? For example, do I tell myself that other people do not treat me fairly enough, that people frustrate me too much, or that people should always treat me in a pleasant, convenient, and satisfying way? Do I tell myself that I should be a special person who should never be treated unsatisfactorily by others?

c) Why do I believe that I *must* or *should* be treated in the way I have stated above? Do I believe that when people disappoint me, criticize me, frustrate me, reject me, they are making me a worthless person or they are making my life unbearable?

d) *Where is the evidence that:* I *must* or *should* always be treated satisfactorily by people? I should be or can be a special person who should be treated better than other people or be treated in a completely satisfactory way? I am no good or my life is terrible and unbearable when I am disappointed, criticized, frustrated, or rejected by other people?

e) What would be a realistic belief to hold about myself and my life in view of the fact that many people will disappoint me, criticize me, frustrate me, or reject me, and some people will do so most of the time?

f) How can I begin to act today toward my co-workers, my peers, my family and friends so that I can enjoy life and give meaning to it despite the unpleasant way that some people presently treat me?

4 As a child, did I interpret my parents' behavior to mean that many things in life are difficult and ungratifying and that commitment, hard work, self-honesty, responsibility, and a belief in the future are essential if I am to give meaning to my life? Or did I interpret their behavior to mean that life should be simple, easy, unfrustrating, and that commitment, hard work, self-honesty, responsibility, and a belief in the future are either irrelevant or

To look at ourselves 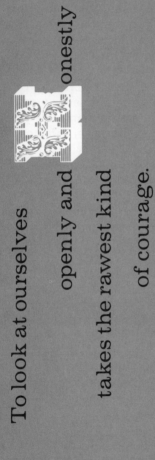onestly openly and takes the rawest kind of courage.

disadvantageous in having a meaningful and satisfying life?

a) What evidence did I have that my interpretation of my parents' behavior was accurate?

b) What do I tell myself today about *needing* an easy and totally enjoyable life? For example, do I tell myself that I should not have to work hard to achieve goals, that being honest and responsible should be easy, that I should never be frustrated or disappointed, that life should always please me? Do I tell myself that I should be a special person who should have a special life?

c) Why do I believe that I *must* or *should* have the easy life that I have stated above? Do I believe that I am no good or that my life is unbearable if I have to work and suffer like other people? Do I believe that life should be meaningful and rewarding without making commitments, without being honest and responsible, and without believing in and working for a future?

d) *Where is the evidence that:* My life *must* or *should* be simple, easy, and painless? I should or can be a special person? Meaning and satisfaction should be experienced in life without making commitments, without being honest and responsible, and without working for a future? I am no good or my life is awful and unbearable when my situation is difficult and ungratifying at times?

e) What would be a realistic belief to hold about myself and my life in view of the fact that life is often difficult and frustrating?

f) How can I begin to act today at work, at school and at home so that I can enjoy life and give meaning to it despite its disappointments and difficulties?

Conquering irrational fears

People find greater satisfaction in life not only by formulating a more realistic philosophy of life but also by working to conquer their irrational fears (fears of situations or activities that in reality produce no harm). Perhaps the irrational fears that people most often want to conquer are those affecting their interactions with others.

Behind practically every irrational fear, whether it is of being honest with another, speaking in front of a group or being intimate with a member of the opposite sex, is the *perfectionistic demand* that one perform flawlessly and be totally accepted and approved. A person who makes this demand believes that failures, criticism or rejection can make one no good and make life terrible.

People are afraid to be honest in their relationships because they believe that total honesty would be catastrophic. They believe that revealing their thoughts, dislikes, imperfections, weaknesses, and mistakes, especially to a companion, would either make them awful or endanger all that is important to them. If a girl is afraid to tell her boyfriend that she dislikes being called on the telephone late at night, or that she does not want to engage in premarital sex, she most likely believes that her honesty might upset her boyfriend. She further believes that a) if she upset her boyfriend, she would be a terrible person, b) if he becomes upset, he will reject her and c) if she is rejected, she will never find another great boyfriend and her entire life will be miserable. She could dispute her self-talk in the following ways:

Where is the evidence that I will be a terrible person for telling my boyfriend about my dislikes? If I communicate with "I don't like" statements rather than with "you are" statements, I have no logical reason for believing that I am being unkind. If my boyfriend becomes upset over my dislikes, that's *his* problem not mine. I have a right to state my likes and dislikes, and I am not responsible for his reaction to them. I can never *make him* (or anyone else) upset any more than other people *make me* upset. My boyfriend will *make himself* upset because he will be telling himself that I shouldn't say the things that I am saying.

Also, where is the evidence that telling my boyfriend I dislike late night phone calls or pre-marital sex will lead to rejection and a miserable life? To be sure, my boyfriend may become irritated by my honesty, but I have no proof that he will reject me. And let's assume the worst. Let's assume that my boyfriend *does* reject me. How does my life become miserable if I am rejected? In fact, if my boyfriend rejects me because of my honesty, won't I discover that an open and realistic relationship could not really develop with him? And if *one* man rejects me because of my honesty, is this evidence that *every* man will reject me? To be sure, not all men will like me for being honest, but my beliefs and traits are valued by some of them. I *can* find more than one man whom I can like and who can like me (and my honesty).

Identifying and challenging irrational self-talk may be insufficient to eradicate the fear of interacting with others. A more effective method is to make a double-barreled attack on the fear by 1) challenging the irrational idea that mistakes, criticism or rejection are horrible or catastrophic and 2) doing the things that are feared in *graduated* steps. *Doing* is the surest way to *prove to oneself* that one will *not* collapse and that the world will *not* end when one makes mistakes or is criticized or rejected.

If a young person is afraid to date because he or she fears rejection, the following suggestions may prove helpful: Keep a small notebook and pencil during the day to record every occasion that you were afraid to ask someone for a date. At night review all the occasions and complete a rational self-counseling worksheet on each one. Then specify and carry out a rational action strategy such as: During the first week, approach at least four different members of the opposite sex and talk with them about anything—directions to a part of town, the time of day, a place to board a downtown or uptown bus. During the second week, talk again with at least four different possible dates and ask at least two of them to have coffee or a drink. During the third week, make at least one date. If a request for a date is met with a "No," keep asking different persons for dates until you get at least one "Yes." Do this for six consecutive weeks.

Someone who is afraid to speak before a group can eradicate this fear by making the two-pronged attack of 1) identifying and challenging irrational self-talk and 2) deciding on and carrying out specific, graduated speaking assignments. That is, completing an RSC work-sheet on the fear, and then specifying and carry-ing out a rational action strategy like the follow-ing assignments done four or five days apart:

1 Ask one or two questions at a lecture or meeting.
2 Express your point of view once or twice in a meeting or discussion group.
3 Speak out several times in a group.
4 Moderate a small discussion group.
5 Moderate a large discussion group.
6 Give a short talk to a small group.
7 Give a long talk to a small group.
8 Give a short talk to a large group.
9 Give a long talk to a large group.

In the Fall 1973 issue of *Rational Living,* Albert Ellis suggests that if one avoids implementing rational action strategies such as the preceding graduated speaking assignments, it is important to identify and challenge the irrational self-talk that interferes with the completion of the assign-ments. One can ask and answer questions like:

When I thought of speaking, what did I tell myself before I withdrew?
What terrible things did I think would happen?
What evidence can I use to challenge my irrational self-talk?
What can I tell myself the next time I begin to feel anxious about speaking so that I can prevent anxiety from interfering with the completion of my speaking assignments?

One device that may be helpful in controlling anxiety before an event or activity is to exaggerate the feared consequences to a *ridiculous* degree. This technique enables one to recognize in a humorous way that nothing truly awful will happen. George, a male college student whom I saw recently, was so afraid of what people would think about his mild stuttering problem that he refused to speak before a class. Yet he wanted to become a teacher. After he learned to do the four steps of RSC, I gave him six graduated speaking assignments. I also instructed him to do the following: "Each time you find that you are anxious as you prepare to do one of the assignments I have given you, imagine that you have just begun to speak before a large audience and each of the following things is happening:

1 all members of the audience laugh, boo and walk out;
2 a banner is placed on the front of each house and office building around the world reading, GEORGE IS A POOR SPEAKER;
3 all newspapers in America and abroad have as their front page headline, GEORGE STUTTERS;
4 all radio and television stations interrupt all of their scheduled programming every half hour to announce that GEORGE CAN'T TALK PERFECTLY;
5 every five minutes an airplane flies above each town around the world and writes out with black smoke, LOOK OUT FOR GEORGE!

You are then to tell yourself, 'That is what "terrible" could mean. Now what is the probability that these "terrible" things are really going to happen to me?' "

By using this technique in conjunction with RSC worksheets, George found that he became relaxed before each speech. As a consequence, he stuttered little with his first speech and stuttered less and less with each subsequent speech. After eight counseling sessions with me over an eight week period, he neither stuttered nor feared speaking before a group.

It cannot be overemphasized that a fear cannot be eradicated by avoidance. On the contrary, the avoidance of fearful situations usually increases fear because avoidance prevents people from gathering reliable and persuasive evidence that they have nothing to fear. Without evidence to dispute their irrational fears, they harbor them with more conviction each passing day. Only by gradually doing the things they are afraid to do can people overcome their fears.

The successful elimination of irrational fears requires acceptance of personal responsibility for *making oneself afraid. Unless physical force is used, people make themselves do whatever they do and that includes making themselves unduly afraid or anxious.* When they reject responsibility for their irrational fears, they say to themselves: "He (or she) made me upset." "It made me upset." "I let him (or her) upset me." "I let it upset me." People who accept responsibility tell themselves,

I made myself upset.

At the same time, honestly accept responsibility for *actively working to eradicate* irrational fears. This means 1) identifying and challenging irrational self-talk and 2) practicing the feared activity in graduated steps. It is important to remember that *a RSC worksheet is not a substi-*

tute for rational action. In order to eliminate unhappiness through rational self-counseling, it is essential to *implement* specific, concrete, rational action strategies. It is also important not to confuse the *wish* to try out a strategy with the *act* of trying it out. All too often people tell themselves that they are really trying when in fact they are merely *thinking* about acting.

> Trying is doing specific, concrete,
> rational acts, and doing them,
> not haphazardly once or twice,
> but systematically and repeatedly,
> improving what can be improved
> and accepting what cannot.

Being unafraid in interactions with others is not easy. But, by practicing rational self-counseling and carrying out specific concrete rational action strategies or assignments each day, one will become less and less afraid regarding personal relationships because one will gradually recognize that regardless of personal thoughts, dislikes, imperfections, weaknesses and mistakes and regardless of other people's reactions, one is never less than a fallible human being who can always give meaning to and enjoy life.

Helping
a companion

Almost everyone knows someone who acts in an irritating and annoying way. It may be that this unpleasant person is a parent, a spouse, a son or daughter. Helping such a person to be less unpleasant and less unhappy is very difficult. However, the following suggestions may reduce or possibly eliminate the objectionable behavior.

A person who is angry, depressed or otherwise upset over another's behavior cannot hope to persuade that other to talk to himself or herself in a more rational way. Therefore, regardless of whether one is a parent, spouse, son, daughter, or in some other role, the first task in helping someone is to rationally manage one's own emotional reactions toward the other's behavior.

The most important rule in managing these reactions is to avoid *"awfulizing" about the other person's behavior.* A wife could avoid "awfulizing" over her husband's behavior by telling herself, "I don't like Bill's behavior, but he is not terrible when he behaves the way he does. Nor am I worthless when he mistreats me. Bill can never make me no good even though he ignores me or calls me all kinds of foul names. Nor is my life situation unbearable. There are many enjoyable things to do, and I can spend my time doing them instead of making myself upset over Bill's unpleasant behavior.

A second rule in managing emotional reactions is to *avoid personalizing another's behavior.* Even when someone deliberately goes out of the way to be unpleasant, it is false to believe that such an individual is personally antagonistic. In reality the person is against *himself* or *herself* and strongly believes that he or she is no good and that life is unbearable. And since the individual erroneously believes that *others* can *make* one worthless or *make* life unbearable, the person lashes out at other people.

A third rule is to *unconditionally accept the person.* If the wife in the previous example were to accept Bill unconditionally, she would tell herself, "Bill is acting in this angry, selfish, or dishonest way because he is telling himself irrational things about himself and the world. He is not an evil person but a confused person, and confused people generally act in angry, selfish and dishonest ways. When he learns more realistic beliefs about himself and his life, he won't be acting this way."

As Albert Ellis points out in *How to Live With a Neurotic,* it is not easy to accept an unpleasant person. But if one hopes to persuade the person to change, full and unconditional acceptance is essential.

A fourth step in managing emotional reactions is to refuse to have *expectations of good behavior* from the other person. *Expectations are what set people up to make themselves angry or depressed.* Keep in mind that an *expectation* is a *demand* that things happen the way a person wants them to happen. Thus, if one becomes angry or depressed over the way another is behaving, it is because one is demanding that the person not do the things that one objects to. Remember that a confused and unhappy person is not open, honest, responsible, reliable, appreciative, sharing, or anything else that is generally found in a person who thinks and acts rationally. Instead, such an individual tends to be hostile, evasive, ungrateful, self-centered and unloving. To expect a confused person to behave in any way except unpleasantly is to invite emotional upsets. Therefore, every time one is disappointed with another's behavior, it is rational to

Perfection

Not

as a final goal,

but the ever-enduring

process

of perfecting,

maturing,

refining,

is the aim of living.

say "Why *should* anyone behave the way *I want* rather than the way *he or she has learned to behave over many years?* Why *shouldn't* a person who believes many irrational things be selfish, hostile, unloving and otherwise unpleasant?

After learning to manage emotional reactions, one can take steps to help the confused person examine and modify his or her behavior. An important first step is to *avoid blaming.* It is advisable to avoid blaming for two reasons. First, the confused person does not *wish* to be confused. Confusion was not chosen as a way of life. As a child, one unwittingly learns some unrealistic ways of thinking and acting. The parents could be blamed, but they too were confused and did not know what they were doing. Second, blame will only exacerbate the confusion. A person who is blamed for behaving irrationally will damn himself or herself for being irrational. And the self-damning will only lead to more confusion and unhappiness.

Another important rule is *to avoid bullying.* Trying to bully a person into giving up irrational beliefs may be threatening, and it is likely that even more irrational behavior will result. Irrational beliefs will be abandoned only when one recognizes the truth about one's life and realizes that it is advantageous to make life choices in terms of the truth. A climate that encourages the discovery and acceptance of the truth is created not by bullying but by understanding.

Another important rule in helping is *to avoid criticizing the confused individual as a person.* People become confused and unpleasant largely from being judged as bad persons by parents during early childhood. Parental criticism has taught children to criticize *themselves* for each of their poor performances and mistakes. Severely criticized children tend to become adults who believe they *must* perform perfectly. When they make mistakes, they tell themselves that they are no good. They tend to interpret criticism as evidence of their worthlessness. They can often be helped if one responds in a forgiving manner when mistakes are made.

The ultimate objective is to help the confused person give up the following irrational beliefs:

1 A person has to perform in a perfect way.
2 Mistakes, criticism, or rejection make a person worthless.
3 A person has to be treated in a totally satisfactory way.
4 Disappointments, frustrations, betrayals or losses make one's life terrible and not worth living.

It is not possible to help persons become less confused and unpleasant simply by telling them that their beliefs are irrational. They require help to discover what they are telling themselves and to ferret out and dispute the self-sabotaging beliefs. Irrational beliefs will be abandoned only when people prove to themselves that they are not failures and that mistakes, disappointments, frustrations or losses do not make them no good and do not make their lives awful and unbearable.

There are two ways to help people gather the evidence needed to develop more accurate views about their lives.

First,

someone who is afraid to do a certain thing,

believing that failure will probably result and that failure will be disastrous, can be induced to become *gradually* involved with the action that is feared.

As stated earlier in the chapter, with gradual involvement and practice, the individual will acquire more knowledge and skill, and these in turn will provide evidence that *total* failure does not exist in *anything.*

Praising an individual's efforts to improve behavior can help a confused person. The husband who would like his wife to realize that she is not a failure in the kitchen can take the first opportunity that arises to compliment her cooking—when she does a better job than usual or successfully tries a new recipe. She is likely to respond to this encouragement and try again. Chances are, if her husband continues to recognize and praise his wife's efforts, she will actually improve her cooking skills. When things do not turn out as she desires, she can be shown that a) she is not a failure and can never be less than a fallible human being and b) she can do many productive and enjoyable things despite her limitations.

Second,

acting rationally in the face of failure and other events that the confused person interprets as catastrophic can make one an effective model, demonstrating that one is never less than a fallible person and can always have a meaningful and satisfying life regardless of the unpleasantness experienced.

However, if one "awfulizes," the confused person may simply say that this is proof that life's problems *are* awful and unmanageable. Whether one's personal behavior provides a rational model can be discovered by asking, "Do I become depressed or collapse every time I fail at a task? Do I become angry when confronted with too many things to do at once? Do I go into a rage when a mistake happens? Do I become highly critical when a neighbor or co-worker has treated me in an unpleasant way? If the answer to these questions is "yes," the confused person is being shown that it is appropriate to: a) *demand* that people and situations be the way one likes them to be, and b) *make* oneself *upset* when people and situations fail to be exactly the way one prefers. The best kind of a model for a confused and unpleasant person is a calm and non-angry one, stating complaints without blaming and without "awfulizing." No amount of preaching to a confused person about the importance of talking rationally to oneself will be very convincing unless the preacher *acts* rationally.

Finally, if one chooses to work each day to encourage a person to think and act more rationally, it is wise to do so without any expectations. Expecting a person to change or expecting payment for time and effort is irrational. *Nobody is under any obligation to change.* As Ellis points out in *A Guide To Rational Living:*

> Although we do have the power to change and
> control ourselves to a considerable degree (if we
> work hard and long enough at modifying our own
> beliefs and actions), we do not have a similar
> power to control the behavior of others. No
> matter how wisely we may counsel others, they
> are still independent entities and may—and
> indeed, have the right as individuals—to choose
> to ignore us completely.

In conclusion, most people will discover that hard work and daily practice are essential to eliminate the self-defeating ideas and habits that were acquired since childhood. Unfortunately, many individuals believe that they can have a more meaningful and satisfying life without working to create it. Some people dislike their jobs, but they will not make the effort to go back to school or to retrain for a different occupation. Some people dislike their marriage, but they will not make the effort to discover and use more honest and rational ways of communicating and satisfying the wants in their relationship. Often the people who refuse to *improve* their life situation also refuse to *accept* it. They want to have a highly satisfying life, and they want it magically without *any work or compromises.* However, there is no short cut or magic to creating a meaningful and satisfying life. Hard work is required to change the circumstances that are changeable and to accept and live with the unpleasant circumstances that cannot be changed.

seven

Getting professional help

seven

Rational self-counseling may not be sufficient to help people deal realistically with the problems of daily living. If they cannot solve their problems and relieve their unhappiness by themselves, they may want to get help from a trained psychotherapist. However, this can be difficult and disappointing. Psychotherapists are somewhat like public officials. Each has his own beliefs; each implements his own set of problem-solving techniques, and each is confident about being able to help people deal with the complexities of life. Therefore it is extremely important to obtain as much useful and reliable information as is possible. Otherwise, as Daniel Wiener points out in *A Practical Guide to Psychotherapy,* one will be "at the mercy of the most persuasive propagandist, the most readily available service, the most effective indirect advertising, or the most compelling advice of friends and strangers."

While there is no precise way of selecting a therapist, there are several steps that can be taken to gather sufficient information to make a sound decision.

First,

draw up a list of therapists within a reasonable commuting distance.

Any institution or agency that directly or indirectly uses the services of personnel in psychology or psychiatry is a good place to search for names. The chairman of the psychology department of a local college or university often can provide the names of therapists or make referrals to someone who can. Hospitals, child guidance clinics and social work offices are also good places to inquire about therapists.

Second,

gather reliable information about the qualifications and performance record of each therapist on the list. Specifically, it is important to know the following information about each therapist:

1 *Competence:* To what degree is this therapist a skilled practitioner in the specific problem area? Are there problems he or she is unwilling or unable to handle? What are his or her biases and blind spots?

2 *Method of operation:* What specific methods are used to help clients learn to manage their own lives? Are clients kept fully informed? How often are contacts made with clients? What are the fees?

3 *Ethics:* To what degree does this therapist engage in honest, confidential and responsible practices with clients?

Where can such information be obtained? Three helpful sources of information about the professional qualifications of a therapist are (1) biographical directories and certification lists, (2) ex-clients, and (3) the therapist.

The Biographical Directory of Fellows and Members of the American Psychiatric Association and the *Directory of the American Psycho-*

Not everything

that is faced

can be Changed;

but nothing

can be

changed

until it is faced.

logical Association may indicate whether the therapists on the list meet the minimal requirements of a reputable certifying agency for clinical competence. A psychologist who has been certified by the American Board of Examiners in Professional Psychology has the initials ABPP in his professional biography. However, biographical directories do not indicate the kind of training a therapist has received or the areas of specialization.

The certifying agency for clinical competence in Rational Therapy is the Institute for Advanced Study in Rational Psychotherapy, a training and certifying center chartered by the Regents of the University of the State of New York. The Institute has a list of certified rational therapists practicing throughout the country. This list can be obtained by writing to Institute for Advanced Study in Rational Psychotherapy, 45 East 65th Street, New York, N.Y. 10021.

A helpful way to judge the competence, method of operation and ethics of each therapist is to determine his or her reputation with clients. Those currently in therapy can provide valuable information about a therapist, although they may give distorted, exaggerated or incomplete accounts of their therapy experience. Thus it is wise to interpret their opinions carefully and ask them to substantiate their claims. Daniel Wiener suggests that ex-clients, though difficult to find, may be the best source of information about what is likely to happen with a particular therapist. If one is fortunate enough to locate ex-clients, it would be very worthwhile to have a candid and thorough discussion with them about their therapy experience. It is better to talk with clients who have terminated therapy for several months. Since the personal relationship with the therapist has ended, they are likely to have a more realistic perspective on the help they have received. Bear in mind that ex-clients may give an unreliable account of their therapy experience. They may blame an effective therapist for their own unwillingness to do the work and practice prescribed in therapy, or they may idealize an ineffective therapist because they believe it would be humiliating to admit that an enormous amount of their time and money was wasted.

Having an interview strictly for informational purposes may be the best guide for selecting a therapist. Although it may not be possible to determine success rate or likely effectiveness from a single interview, the discussion will indicate whether it would be worth working with the therapist for a trial period at least. One can decide which therapists to interview by using the information gathered from biographical directories, the list of rational therapists, and ex-clients to reduce the list of potential therapists to three.

When interviewing each therapist, it is important to have a clear idea of the specific facts that one wants to discover. While the initial interview is not the time to present problems and ask for advice and solutions, it is advisable to have a tentative list of questions to ask before the meeting in order to gather the specific information desired.

Follow the advice that Roger Golde gives in *Can You Be Sure of Your Experts?:* get the therapist on record *before* going into much detail about personal problems. Without revealing the kind of answers one is seeking, discover the therapist's beliefs about the causes of most personal problems, the methods employed to help clients solve their problems, the kinds of problems dealt with most (and least), the problem areas he or she is least qualified to handle, the type of clients seen, the frequency of therapy sessions, fees, the types of problems referred to others, to whom clients are referred, etc.

Keep in mind that the therapist often tries to get the client on record first. This ploy can be handled simply by bouncing the ball back into the therapist's lap with something like, "I do have some particular things that I want to discuss about myself, but before I go into that, I'd like to know a little more about the way you work."

When the therapist gives information about methods be sure that it is understood. Understanding can be checked by restating in question form the ideas that the therapist has expressed. For example, one can say, "Let me see if I understand. You mean that . . . ?"

At some time during the interview, it is desirable to present a small problem or situation to the therapist and spend a few minutes discussing it to see how it is handled. The best sample problem is an uncomplicated one that has been recently solved.

Even if some notes have been taken during the interview, it is advisable to write down all reactions to and impressions of the therapist as soon as possible after leaving the office. Do not try to organize a neat list of impressions because doing so will most likely inhibit the flow of ideas. They can be arranged by topic later. Also, do not make any judgments about any of the therapists

The future
will be 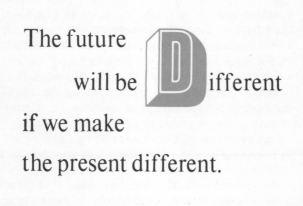ifferent
if we make
the present different.

until there is a chance to write a complete list of impressions and reflect on all three.

After interviewing all three therapists, compare the information from each interview. The following questions can help to evaluate each therapist:

1 How did the therapist respond to me? Was I viewed as another "case" or as a person? Was there real interest in my type of problem? Was the response open and direct or evasive? Was there annoyance with my inquiries into the therapist's skills, values, biases and other particulars in working with clients?

2 How competent did the therapist seem to be in my problem area? What information was I given about methods that would suggest that I can be helped?

3 Approximately how much time will I be in therapy? What will the services probably cost me?

It is important to select a therapist who will help find direct solutions to personal problems. Many therapists believe that both diagnosis and treatment involve deep analysis which is both time-consuming and very expensive. They do not believe that personal problems can be adequately solved unless they analyze all early developments and examine the most remote feelings. Their goal is to help people understand their childhood experiences on the assumption that if and when they do, they will be able to solve their personal problems effectively.

To be sure, analysis of one's early development will provide many insights about the roots of fears and problems. However, insights gained into the past will not *automatically* solve *current* problems. The task of learning to talk to oneself in a rational way and of replacing current self-defeating behavior patterns with more productive and satisfying ones still remains. In short, unless a person wants long-term and very expensive therapy with results that may not satisfy, it is wise to select a therapist who will effectively help one deal directly with the problems that present difficulty each day. If one is unable to find a local therapist who will be of assistance in discovering direct solutions to problems, it would be wise to write to the Institute For Advanced Study in Rational Psychotherapy for referral.

After selecting a therapist, monitor the first few therapy sessions to determine whether they are, in fact, encouraging more productive day-to-day living. More specifically, it is important to ask each of the following questions during the initial sessions:

1 Am I convinced that the therapist is willing to work with me until I learn to deal effectively with my problem?

2 Am I learning to identify and challenge some of the self-defeating beliefs that I hold about myself and my life?

3 Am I being given specific homework assignments designed to help me practice rational self-counseling more effectively than I was able to practice before I decided to undergo therapy?

After several sessions, ask and answer such questions as:

1 Am I discovering how I have been making myself unhappy?

2 Am I learning to believe that I am never a worthless person and that I can always give meaning to my life?

3 Am I learning effective and satisfying ways of dealing with the unpleasant people and events that I encounter?

Do not assume that therapists know everything there is to know about personal problems. Although therapists take many courses in their professional training and pass many tests on what they have learned, their experiences are sometimes inadequate to help with specific problems. Many people go to therapists for help with sexual problems. Yet very few training programs require psychologists or psychiatrists to have extensive knowledge about sexual conflicts and about rational ways for dealing with such conflicts. As a result, some therapists have less knowledge about sex matters than some of their clients.

Counseling deficiencies exist in the handling of other problems. As Daniel Wiener points out, therapists simply did not and could not receive comprehensive training in *all* of the special problems that people have. Since a person's therapist may not know what is best, it is wise to interact intelligently with him and find the best ways for oneself.

Finding the best ways means that during therapy one does not abandon the process of rational self-counseling. Though a therapist may not know the details of this process, it is important to keep using it. Most likely one's therapist will not only encourage the continued use of rational self-counseling but will suggest additional problem-solving strategies.

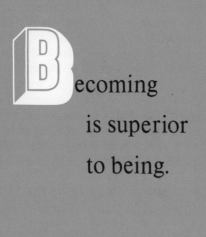

Becoming
is superior
to being.

During therapy it is often helpful to read about the possible causes of and solutions to one's problems. But most of the available reading materials do not offer solutions to personal problems. In my judgment, the most sensible and useful book to read and *re-read* is *A Guide to Rational Living* by Albert Ellis and Robert Harper. It can be purchased as a paperback from Wilshire Book Company, 12015 Sherman Rd., No. Hollywood, California 91605. Two other books that are highly recommended and available from the same publisher are *A Guide to Successful Marriage* and *How to Raise An Emotionally Healthy Happy Child*. These books can also be obtained from The Institute for Advanced Study in Rational Psychotherapy, 45 East 65th Street, New York, New York 10021.

Self-help groups can be extremely valuable during therapy. Especially recommended are the ART groups (Associated Rational Thinkers) which are sponsored by Dr. Maxie Maultsby of the Department of Psychiatry at the University of Kentucky Medical School in Lexington, Kentucky. Information about ART groups is available from ART National Headquarters, 117 W. Main Street, Madison, Wisconsin 53703. These ART groups are rational self-counseling groups and are often better than most of the self-help groups such as Alcoholics Anonymous, Addicts Anonymous, Synanon.

Since a self-help group requires its members to be open and honest with each other, it encourages people to accept and solve their problems within the context of their total environment. In view of the heavy costs of private psychotherapy, it is simple logic for a person to make use of self-help groups such as ART whenever possible to shorten time in therapy.

It is wise to evaluate progress in therapy continually, not simply in terms of how one feels but, more importantly, in terms of how realistically one solves problems and enjoys life. Regardless of what is discovered about the specific *causes* of problems, a person's original goal of *solving* them and giving meaning and satisfaction to life is still the most important consideration. If a husband's problem is sexual impotence with his wife, he may discover in the process of therapy that his wife, mother, and other women try to dominate him and that he would be better off being assertive with aggressive women. While this insight is important, the husband would do well to keep in mind that his goal remains the same—that of engaging in mutually satisfying sexual intercourse with his wife.

> In order to profit from therapy,
> it is essential to continually
> evaluate one's progress
> in terms of the positive changes
> in personal behavior.

If very little progress is made with a therapist or if over a period of time one picks up most of the therapist's know-how without learning how to solve the problem, it may be time to find another therapist. Obviously, the desire for results is to be balanced against the fact that changing long-established beliefs and behavior patterns requires patience and that immediate results sometimes cannot be obtained. Moreover, it is helpful to keep in mind that there is no super

guru or master therapist who will put it all together or who will lead one to all that is true and
good and protect one from all that is false and
evil. All therapists are traveling this same road
that others are traveling as fallible and limited
human beings.

Finally, it is wise to examine personal efforts to
make therapy work. Recognize that ultimately
each individual must assume responsibility for
making progress in dealing with personal problems. If one's intention is simply to attend
therapy sessions, to talk freely and then to wait
for "big things" to happen, one will be sadly
disappointed. Time in therapy has no demon-
strable relationship with behavior change. One
has to set specific, realistic and meaningful
goals, and one has to work hard in small but
concrete steps in order to develop more productive ways of thinking and behaving. The individual who wants to solve personal problems must
make things happen.

> What one gets out of therapy or,
> for that matter, what one gets
> out of anything in life
> is in the first and last analysis
> determined by the individual—by what
> the person is willing to establish
> as a goal
> and work hard at achieving.

Possible rational self-counseling worksheet

1 Unpleasant situation	**3 Rational challenges**

1 Unpleasant situation

My behavior; other people's behavior; unfortunate circumstances

2 Self-talk

A. The awful things my situation signifies

B. The things that should happen

3 Rational challenges

Challenging my opinion of situation

Is my opinion true?

Challenging my self-talk

(Is my self-talk true? Where is the evidence? What am I exaggerating? What grandiose or perfectionistic demands am I making? What kind of self-talk will best help me understand my situation and eliminate emotional upsets and interpersonal conflicts?)

4 Rational action strategy

(What kind of strategy will best help me improve the things that can be improved in my situation and accept the things that cannot?)